# narrat
# enigma /
## rumours uv
## hurricane

# bill bissett

**Talonbooks**
**2004**

Talonbooks
P.O. Box 2076, Vancouver, British Columbia, Canada V6B 3S3
www.talonbooks.com

Typeset in Librarian and printed and bound in Canada by Hignell
Book Printing.

First Printing: July 2004

**Library and Archives Canada Cataloguing in Publication**

Bissett, Bill, 1939–
    Narrativ enigma/rumours uv hurricane / Bill Bissett.

Poems.
ISBN 0-88922-507-9

    I. Title.

PS8503.I78N37 2004    C811'.54    C2004-903253-4

The publisher gratefully acknowledges the financial support of the
Canada Council for the Arts; the Government of Canada through
the Book Publishing Industry Development Program; and the
Province of British Columbia through the British Columbia Arts
Council for our publishing activities.

Canadä

**much thanks 2**   th leeg uv canadian poets   th writrs yunyun
**steve clay**  granary books new york  pteros art gallery **virginia**
**dickson** n **randy resch** 4 art show **vishyuns uv being**  toronto
 th art collektors   th federaysyun uv canadian writrs  th poetree
venues  this aint th rosedale libraree bookstore  toronto **jena**
**hamilton & dr joy masuhara** van **jonathan rainbow & michel**
**potvin  n  dr bill berinati**  toronto  n red deer press calgary
bc book prizes 4 dorothy livesay award 4 peter among th
towr ing  boxes (Talonbooks)   all much thanks thanks 2

publikaysyns **unarmd** mineapolis   **descant** toronto  **capilano**
**review** *north vancouvr* **bill bissett**  guernica  editions  toronto
**linda rogers** ed   from paris **100 poets against th war  todd**
**swift** ed salt publishing australia **common sky darren wershler**
**-henry  & mark higgins & stephen pender** eds toronto


**bill roberts**   4 whos mewsik on  ***rumours uv hurricane  cd***
(red deer)  th following texts wer writtn   rumours uv hurricane
th road  desert wings   seasons uv th heart  jaguar jumps   yu
know iuv got shares in paradise  //  aria 4 isis  n  ths room is
still heer  also  wer writtn 2 his mewsik  not yet recordid

**th oranges uv orantangua**  hous press  **derek beaulieu   ed**
calgary   in wch th oranges uv orantangua   i want 2 b emptee
thers snow in orangevile  i dreemd i livd with keanu reeves n
sum othr pomes heer wer first  printid  ltd edition 80 copeez

n thanks 2 linda rogers who sd ' also remembr we ar th bone
peopul thos carree us thru ' from  pome 'jeff sd i embrace
th messeeness uv life'

dont yu think
life is strange

can yu describe
what els
ther is

## i herd th toastr titul sing in my
## masculine reveree

i herd th toastr sing ths morning  a rathr mourn
ful sound      valise  valees   VA LEES
what  erthlee meening cud that impart  i had no
idea

n i cud heer furthr  as i sippd on my grapefruit juis
th elevatora  goez  boof  BOOF  outside n down th
hall  thn  kreeklee n splatchlee  n a possibul figur
approaching  on th slitelee staind hall karpeting   pit
pall papal popal opal pipul pifful papal  opa  opo lo ap l
polo  pipul pafful  popal  papal palap  pa lips al  olo lo op
lop pop pap pap a popal a papal pull up  papal  popal
poop popal  papal  pip   ip  papal pipul   pal pal  po op po
ooop loop   pool     ap  ap  pa  apo  lop a   o    loop

a size uv loafr   prhaps a littul 2 large 4 th weerer
had sumwun resentlee just left
door knok
i opend

i walkd back a bit as he enterd n thn he approachd me
konsepts whirling in my hed   inside  outside  singing
toastrs  intensyunal follee  papal pollee
he moovd tord me   touching my nippuls
n sd as he pulld me tord him   n down
my name is matthew poindexter

at second blush i rathr doubtid ths sweet assersyun
as he n i nevr met b4  arrangd n sought a love 4 our
selvs in th desolate world n war weeree envelope uv
time n space        wud th elevator go bonf  BONF
agen     th grapefruit cud wait

## th oranges uv
## orantangua

brout me th magik  uv
being closr with yu
fairlee soon aftr first
tasting  its orange

liquid n meet pouring
thru my lips opn
mouth

th problematiks uv wishings
rathr thn th findings        n eye
marvel  why dont i dew ths
all th time it takes 2 find
2 fit it in  2 satisfy our
reel needs

rathr thn how eye
draft  drift  distrakt     obsess
enjoy   all thees fabulous
diamonds nd
precious stones uv being
opulent optiks  th
kontinuing  epiphaneez uv
each day  n
milieu  rathr  thn th
fabulous delays  being
n  finding it        ducking
th big konstrukts  n
each time        ths wun

agen  thees parts uv  maneeness
how i love him

n accepting th parametrs
uv letting go  n  on
2 th next     errands

6

memoreez uv orantang
u a   walking with
me  2 th bordr  wher i

get photographd n

how iuv changd agen
thru th incens  n warm
yang towels  th camera

dusint  recognize me

if they take away our brains weul still remembr if
they take away our minds weul still recall if we find
ourselvs missing weul find each othr aftr all if they
take away our brains weul still remembr if they
take away our minds weul still recall if we find
ourselvs missing weul find each othr aftr all if they
take away our brains weul still remembr if they take
away our minds weul still recall if we find our
selvs missing weul find each othr aftr all if they take
away our brains weul still remembr if they take away
our minds weul still recall if we find ourselvs missing
weul find each othr aftr all

7

## i want 2 b emptee

emptee uv promises
obligaysyuns  appointments n oint
ments 4 a whil  feel th treez
grow in2 my hed n feet
feel th ekstasee  as it cums
4 me  not me running aftr it
foot steps in th gravl n sand
wheeling tord me

i cant remembr my appointments
rite in th qualifying quandree th
needs  2 b bittrsweet

felld by ekstasee
th hand up yr innr thigh  like
a machete thankfulee cutting thru
yr armour  yr building defenses  th
kalsifikaysyuns  on yr
bones  tempt yu 2 arcania n
soaking onlee
emptee uv feer
emptee uv purpose
emptee uv meening a
way in2 desire

de  si re  de ires
ed  de  resi de esir
desi rre  desiraaay  is
that yu   hmmmm
n thn  latr  THER IS A
LATR  wow  eye love my appointments
n ointments  all th meetings n stuff
man its ok reelee

n get back in2 th swimming
amphibian  watr summr saulting
n brest with a touch uv buttrfly
n side n back n th multi
tasking crawl
n th multi  tasking
CRAWL
ium hungree
agen

fill me  fill me  *fill me*

gg
ddddddd ddddb
ᔕᔕᑢᕮᑢᔕᔕᑢᕮᑢᑢᑢᑢᔕᑢ
ﬁﬁﬁﬁﬁﬁ ﬁﬁﬁﬁﬁﬁ ﬁﬁﬁﬁﬁﬁﬁﬁﬁﬁﬁﬁn
ᔕᔕᔕᔕᔕᔕᔕᔕᔕᔕᔕᔕᔕᔕᔕᔕᔕᔕᔕᔕᔕᔕᔕᔕᕮᕮᕮᕮᕮᕮᕮᕮᔕᕮ
ᑳᑳᑳᑳᑳᑳᑳᑳᑳᑳᑳᑳᑳᑳᑳᑳᑳᑳᑳᑳᑳᑳᑳᑳᑳᑳᑳ☒
meet
bred  go sumwher wher thers
ᑳᑳᑳᑳᑳᑳᑳᑳᑳᑳᑳᑳᑳᑳᑳᑳᑳᑳᑳᑳᑳᑳᑳᑳᑳᑳᑳᑳᑳᑳᑳᑳᑳᑳᑳᑳᑳᑳᑳᑳᑳᑳᑳᑳᑳᑳ
xᑳᑳᑳᑳᑳᑳᑳᑳᑳᑳᑳᑳᑳᑳᑳᑳᑳᑳᑳᑳᑳᑳᑳᑳᑳᑳᑳᑳᑳᑳᑳᑳᑳᑳᑳᑳᑳᑳᑳ
ᑳᑳᑳᑳᑳᑳᑳᑳᑳᑳᑳᑳᑳᑳᑳᑳᑳ

fill

me

# jeff sd
## eye embrace th messeeness uv life
## living is  messee  isint it


evn tho i know its easier 2 work in a tidee room  sum
timez yu dew get mor inspiraysyun  in a mess  dont yu

        th squisheeness uv evreething      sailing out
    stelthee n alert thru th wetness uv watr  cloud  n
        fog  coppr mist ovr th strangr waves  will find us
    our acheevments  our misyun  satisfied  our delite


n also our endless murkee wetness  onlee th surface is
                        seeminglee  dryer  uv our face
    say  taybul  if its wiped  wer mooving thru


    hevee   wet  endless  squisheeness  in our breeth
ing   we try 2 keep it trim  n tidee  th sails b4
    th steem  engine  th text box all  kleer uv othr
    copee  not part uv ths message  leeking in  or our
    out  trim  n keep yr powdr dry  how oftn  is it
                            reelee


    well   it can help 4 sure   close yr files documents
b4 shutting down  sews its not a mess whn yu reopn
    houskeeping
                    th nayturs uv habit  n whn we cum
    2 a program agen  its ther  not spilling out uv th
parametrs
            why  hmmmmm  not
                        we ar enklosd
    facing   an othr  enklosures  thru  thees framings we
find  mor opnings  he sd rubbing his hands thru my
                        eyez  ears  n hair

yet uv kours  if its 2 tidy  makes us think  its not
messee  our sours  ora gins  n de part yures onlee
sumtimes  its  kleen

$\qquad$ k  k l l l leen$\qquad$eeeen


getting up  in th infinit wetness  n squisheeness
dreem in it   love in it    listn 2 th heeling voices


in it    gives thanks in it   was it all onlee a shadow


play  start agen$\qquad$anothr voyage   in th huge
squisheenee fog  horns    stoves  boiling ovr
warnings  n take care he sd  n keep going  dew th
best we can  hed up  thru th squishlee dark
$\qquad\qquad\qquad$ th beautiful dark
n follow th kompass
uv yr heart


we need 2 remembr also  linda  sd


we ar th bone peopul


thos carree us  thru


if they take away our brains weul still remembr if
they take away our minds weul still recall  if we find
ourselvs missing  weul find each othr aftr all  if they
take away our brains weul still remembr if they find
away our brains weul still recall if we find
our brains weul still remembr if they take
minds weul still recall if they take away
weul find our brains weul still remember if they take away
weul find ourselvs missing
weul find each othr aftr all

## she sd she was sortuv strange whn
## i askd her how she was     melanie

they wer changing her meds  n ther was sum side
effekts   othrwise  she was fine  she was fine anee
   way  she addid  tho a littul strangelee  a mix
uv wisteria wistfulness n th temptaysyun 2ward
   sum vague undeklarabul sterness who cud know
   certinlee th drilling was getting loudr n loudr

nothing wrong with strange i intrspersd  strange is
alrite  can b  xcellent

   feel th mosyun uv th oysyun

strange is  can b  th axis on wch  turnings  we
   reelee  dew sew much as well   as evn grateful 4
th presiens  grateful 4 th presedentz  4 th joyous
ness  cum in2 me  love it he sd 2 me ium cumm
ing in2 yu  lick it  ths evree moment  is  yuneek

wher is th pattern   have yu reelee seen anee uv
                        ths b4

onlee th eternal  strangeness  beautee  we ar veree
tiny  make big deels  cud chill mor   take it  eezee
have what  17 kilometrs  or is less  uv air 2 breeth
   it in deep  vertikalee  what a galaxee  n raging
ium enjoying th kontinuum uv ths window  whos
walking by  evn i know  its a kreeaysyun uv my
   own mind  soul  spirit  its sew hilarious reelee

      sew cum with me  n feel th mosyun  uv th
osyun   feel th sway uv th tides  th moon beem
barnakuld  lapshurs  silkn  orakul
     n fethr th wethr   gambol th blood is
up n sunning  tormentine     th watchr
     tree trunk  th aperture  widens  lets in mor
lite  evn tho our air home    thats oxygen 2 us
is sew not tall  at all

      he sd  we think thats certintee
n ther isint     we think ther can b
          a roundelay uv
previous prsons n they dont
      its mostlee  all nevr seen b4
        goin by th hous  in all seesyuns
                    in all reesons
          doncha  think    its strange th

    tremoring n klamouring n th emptee taybul
      th farsnips uv napkins   bombardid  by
fanseed    nukleer fetishings       o harold

        th   mercuree

13

# rumours uv hurricane

rumours uv hurricane
rumours uv hurricane
rumours uv hurricane

treez ar flying
yachts ar adrift
watr is turning
ovr  hot n
mor  hot

no time 4 sky
no time 4 see
no time 4 love
no time 4 me

pour anothr dreem
pour anothr scheem
pour anothr me
listn 2 th shell
pour anothr me

treez ar flying
yachts ar adrift
watr is turning
ovr  hot n
mor  hot

pour anothr dreem
pour anothr scheem
pour anothr me

listn 2 th shell
pour anothr me
can yu see me
can yu see me

## th road

ium sew hungree
can i feed my soul

ium sew hungree
can i feed my soul

what am i gonna dew
til i see yu

th streets ar narrow
n sew stuk  mad peopul
n masheens  blow in
my way

met a guy 4 a whil
evreething seemd 2 have
sum say  fluid  fluid

th storm cums n th
loudspeekrs angr n
wher ar yu  keep
goin onn

what am i gonna dew
til i see yu

ium sew hungree
can i feed my soul

ium sew hungree
can i feed my soul
can i feed my soul

# desert wings

th wind is changing evreething
th wind is changing evreething
th wind is changing evreething
th wind is changing evreething

how yr eyez apeer
how th stars shine

how yr eyez apeer
how th stars shine

kaleidoscopik midnite heer
we almost disapeer

kaleidoscopik midnite heer
we almost disapeer

ride with me now  no feer
ride with me now  no feer
ride with me now  no feer
ride with me now  no feer

we lookd in th mirage n saw
ourselvs  laffing n kissing
eye didint think weud find
each othr agen

ride with me now  no feer
ride with me now  no feer
ride with me now  no feer
ride with me now  no feer
ride with me now  no feer

## aria 4 isis

**air ria ria ara is si**  if onlee yu wud phone me  huh
if onlee yu wud cum 2 me  if onlee yu wud  call  what is
2 tangenshul  2 realize  2 see  whn yu feel a suddn feer
what gets yu ther  what gets yu  what gets yu heer
what gets yu ther  did yu dreem uv th goddess  in th
ode 2 isis           let go 2 th gods  who take care uv
us  th spirit beings who help us  ar they ther
in th novakane vallee  eye found yu  on th road 2 isis
in th horshu canyun   i cud heer yu  i cud heer yu
dew yu beleev we have identitee apart from memoree
wher duz our soul go  duz it go  is it alwayze heer
ther  n evreewher  on th go  sew travelling   isis a rivr
undr                    in southrn nebraska
th umbrella uv th galaxee  dew yu feel
th frvour  dew yu feel th kontentment  th whirling n
still being  dew yu feel th love  nitemares uv trains
hurtuling thru th nite  dew yu feel  ignorant thrill
th ride  o isis th summr tides  dew we kling 2  our
talking bears  our sumtimes reluktant monkeez
hold them  sew loos n sew tite       tryin  area  arena
2 get all th furnitur in my room against th door  2
keep th door shut against th tall baritone cummin in
2 strap me   th zeon wear  th fabrik  th tapestree
we ar walking thru  as i know yu sew try 2 cum 2 me
cum 2 me   kiss me all ovr  cum 2 me
along th tangentshul  watr slides  th rivr we know
th rivr we call  opn my eyez       th rivr we dont know
th rivr we dont kno  we cAn change th skripts we inheirit
th see monstrs ar layduling fine  he sd   eyeing th
isis a farming town in northrn saskatchewan    eyeing th
dissolving mountin perls n rainbows glide  if yu  onlee
yu wud phone me  if onlee yu wud cum 2 me  iul weer
aneething yu want  eet aneething yu want me 2  dew anee
thing yu want tho i know thats not kool  aneething  longs
its safe if onlee yu wud call  yu wud call   call  call call

# ths room is still heer

why ths room is still heer
n my memoreez uv yu

why ths bed is still heer
n my memoreez uv me

why ths planet still rolls
n ths dreem still goez on

4evr n yu cum   2 th door
n we go   up in th thundr n

lightning   we soar  on above
th bed thru  th roof n in

2  th moon n  th mewsik
takes us on n on n  b4


th time goez  we ar in  all uv
time  th singing  n th dansing

n our bodeez  sew strong
n our bodeez  sew strong


yu cum 2 th door  why
ths room is still heer

n my memoreez uv yu
why ths bed is still heer

n my memoreez uv me

n ths door we fly thru
n ths door we fly thru
n ths door we fly thru

n ths door we fly thru

n th sky we fly thru

n th sky we fly thru

we fly thru th sky
we fly thru th sky

we fly thru th sky

,0.  .

p p  p  apul   lapal   la  p  al  port  al

tortal p  ooor  lap  l  aa  l
         ort  la      lo  roop
   pal    olo    olp     al  rr  r
portal  ortal    tor  tal  a  lo
     alt  rop   la  torp  prrr  o
lac uv  vocal  oral   rol  o  cal
         ov  lac  val  oc   p  p  o
voro  rov  lac r  roc   o  o
acor a or  ort   ta  al  to   ooooo
     portal  vokalllllaa

19

## magik tempul

at sertin timez
th tempul  apeers  timez uv
great  4bodeing  n is a remindr
warning  we all get thru  evn timez uv
we all get thru  2 sumwher
dew we  or great joyousness  possibul
selebraysyun  th axes  n th
aegis  uv metronomee  n dashlee
th salamandr dreems    leg on  up
log on
th swaying beem
we can see its
ramada like roof
its ways uv kurling th
pillars  th songs
uv its masonree
nevr craks  th viewrs  it rises
slowr thn meditativ
breething from th
volkanik rock
2 yr gayze

empteez  n answrs
yr longings    n thn th
tempul disapeers   is  gone
from yr eyez
n is inside yr heart
n th beem uv its
insistent
pneuma
pneuma
pneuma

## *ya kosha mana hi ya keee*

## **its in th magik books**


th storeez uv yu n me ther is no stedee gig tho we
    dreem uv it inkonsistentlee  n konstantlee
        on ths page we ar fishing  having lernd
    sum nu lines


    on ths othr page  we ar dansing  sew fine
  past th middul uv th books  smiling  inside star
klustrs  we ar still  salvaging n creating th arkitextyur
    uv our souls bodeez
    intrakting  physikalee  n changing  n in th
  beem  uv lites   its in th magik books  curling
    dusting  illuminating  n  fresh  n  ancien
we ar loving
            each othr  n touching  sew
    manee  stars  we ar  parts uv  suddnlee  flying
    suddnlee  not trying      its still like whn
we met by th rivr eglantine  on erth  n blossoms


    spun  from our mouths  moths  eyez  n th
  image  l'image    held us  evn tho we cud try 2
  hurt it  n did  n make up 2 it  n ourselvs  n
  othrs  n n n  n  n  who was  eglantine  can yu
  tell me  n  n  n  sew  on  we cud onlee  let go
    let go     n  b


inside th drawing uv th inn keepr  letting us  in
side  neer th end uv th magik book  wch is veree
similar 2  its beginning  n we slept ther  inside his
xcellent bed n brekfast  within th olive green vol
kano  thru wch we latr flew home  at last resonans

from anne carsons autobiographee uv red

turn th page in th magik book  n yul see th nite uv
                              meteor showrs
turn th next page uv th magik book  n yul find evree
thing yu desire  in th text  n pickshurs  keep turning  n
yu  yul breeth 4 evr  in th hours  uv flowrs  n dreems
      n being  we ar a deeplee flawd specees with moments
            uv sumtimes n unprediktabul greatness


      touch me  letting go th memoreez uv th shadows n
   spites      can sumthing b nowher
      ouch me  in th embrs uv th volkano
      uch me  letting go uv th melankolee abt departid
      frends n lovrs  honor them  n brooding
   sew less   touch me  shussh me  flin flon  arabesque
                        bluushkank  arkapelagooo


n th beem we ride in  we oftn dont need 2 b rushing
                              aneething
      sew manee pages  in th magik books
      sew manee   ages  in th magik books


yu know  it was 2 foggee 2 see th meteorite showrs
   cascading past  erth


      it was 2 foggee 2 see  th dimensyuns uv th maroon
      it was 2 foggee 2 see    cape sew  obscurd 2 us


that didint lessn th wundr  in th deep mist we cud heer
kiyots shifting  almost dansing  almost see a brite star
   thru th cloud densness  painting in th magik books
monarch buttrfly  flies  n othr airee kreetshurs  flying
   masquerade  in th fireplace air inside  we cud sew feel
th nite uv th meteor showrs  tho  foolishlee  hung hed a
   bit  not see it  tho frends  ovr a bit on othr hills  cud
   ar yr hands aching 2 carress love


th meteor showrs  sumwher els  in th magik books


22

look   ther we ar   transparenseez btween time n
genre zones   showing thru th ovrlays   envelopd by
th falling stars   shooting comets   meteor showrings
swooping thru th sky

                              in th magik books
                              we dance 4evr
                              n love 4evr


that nite tho   on th hi hill   th meteor showrs wer
                              obscurd   by fog   we
sertinlee cud feel them erupting past ovr a wayze
dreems uv th safe kastul   th marmaduke n duchess
dropping in 4  t  n kukumbr  peenutbuttrs  sand
                   wiches  it was xquisite eye sd  evree
turn n sure fire xplikaysyun  our bodeez  drenchd
in sun n moon  sew cyklikul  soar ovr th kastul
                   spires    n tallest cedar n spruce treez
n kareen ovr th emerald lake  islands  yes  our
bodeez  sew inside each othr  in th magik books
we danse 4evr  n all love 4evr  its not sew diffikult
   2 opn  our minds melting  inside  each othr  our
spirits  lift

                   if yu want2 see mor
                        turn anothr page

                   if yu want 2 hold mor
                        turn anothr  page

if yu want 2 let go mor     turn anothr page
   if yu want 2 touch mor  turn anothr page
   if yu want 2 feel mor  turn anothr page
            let yrself moov in2 th pickshur

   uv th magik books we ar all in

we ar mammals who weer clothes
wev mostlee lost our fur
we get veree cold without      clothes  n  love

mammals with partlee compewtr  heds
mammals with ortlee  compewtr binaree beds
we may get bettr  signs ar apeering
we may get bettr  signs ar apeering
we may get bettr   signs ar apeering
we may get bettr   signs ar apeering
kompewtr bipolar beds
we may get bettr  signs ar apeering
we may get bettr  signs ar apeering
we may get bettr  signs ar apeering
we may get bettr  signs ar apeering
pewtr n flesh   dayzd intensyunaliteez
we may get bettr  signs ar apeering
we may get bettr  signs ar apeering
we may get bettr  signs ar apeering
we may get bettr  signs ar apeering
we may get bettr  signs ar apeering

bye bye  polar  its th ekuatorial breezes 4 me now

a swathendra uv geomansee  lay waste th tarandareen
a sereez uv doubul u ssss  n what if what yu ar asking
mungwell  4  nevr came  evr  wud yu thn if yu knew
whn evr  n cumming westhausen  abord wer  seeandra
n matelee otergos  sanktifilus wher was mickey mudras
or lasko  whiskul  erdrum  fallantario  klusko  talio
talio whiskalee  pelako  whusko  shhhhhhhhhhhhhh
setting  sail    in th glistning  marjareen

doktor  doktor  yu ar 2 deep  we cannot get 2 sleep

## seesons uv th heart

seesons n timez  moments
    cum n go
                they give sew much
whn they
            cum  n hurt sew much
    whn they  go
its like a medikul mirakul  a reel
        crowd  pleezr
      th great timez    bodee
n soul n being   they cum
    n go    n now is th time
    uv th sun in our hearts    tho
diffrentlee shaped   th fire
n air  how they ar careing
            how they ar  careing


        th timez uv spring  how we
rise upward    n sing


    n run 4 each othr  in th treez
    run 4 each othr  by th ocean
                in th stars


    we get it on    evreewher inside th
margin  lines    n ekstatik spaces in btween
th bridges  runways   n forests


    n on top uv th margin lines  whos
            bordrs  blurring


starting agen  no holds  barrd

*summr*

emblazond sun  endless hot moons
our thighs ar strong
i run 2 yu  ovr n ovr
    th yu changes  th moon duz
  n th sun  n th running
 is diffrent  each time
tho it seems like its
  gonna last    n ths time
            n ths time   b

    lasting  it dusint  mattr
hold me agen            *i run 2 yu*
 hold me agen          *ovr n ovr*
   dance with me     *i run 2 yu*
      agen         *ovr n ovr*
  n  agen         *i run 2 yu*
    n  agen       *i run 2 yu*

  wer dansing agen
    in th hallway
    in th allee
    in th mansyun
  undr th summr moon
  in th fields  in th tall grass

  hot  n endless
    hot  n endless

   catch me agen
  iul alwayze catch yu
   iul always catch yu

embrs  moov
  glow inside  us
th winds shape th fields

  th winds shape th fields
    th dansing mor urgent
    time is a faktor now
    4 at leest th outside

we start 2 moov indoors
  we begin 2 moov inside

    lay by th fire
    lay by th fire

      watch th flames grow
      touch each othr  find th
        slow dance  ar we
          in a trance
        touch each othr

      whn werent we
          in a dance
      in sum trance

    finding our changing
      selvs  burn
              n glow

*indian summr*

th beginning uv th cold winds
th warm winds  how long
did they last  ium
            counting
n it dusint tell
me aneething

sumtimez time is suddnlee
fastr  speeds up  all uv a
    suddn  slows  who knows
        from wher

who knows from wher
who knows from wher

thn th slow lavishing
n suspens   suspens

        thn th slow lavishing
            n suspens  suspens

th beginning uv th cold winds
th warm winds  how long did
    they last     ium counting
        n it dusint tell
me aneething

*wintr*

cum 2 me
iul see yu soon
we can love in th time
warmth is held ovr a bit
we dont know how long
we dont know how long
yet we ride 2gethr
yet we ride 2gethr

its not alwayze
warm
aneemor

sumtimez its a bit cold yu know
a cold wind bites
just a bit at th warmth
wch goez
suggests sumthing els

will we go
will we go  from heer
will we go  from heer

hold me in time
hold yu in time
hold us in time
b4 we go
b4 we go

we ran like th wind 2 get heer
now its 2 late 2 go on
is it 2 late 2 go on
is it 2 late 2 go out

th fire hold us in time
b4 we go

# seesons uv th heart

it cums n goez
alwayze beeting
we dont know from wher
or 2   th seesons uv
th heart  june or
decembr  th bones
twinge  yet we ar dansing
dansing  evn as we prepare
2 leev th dansing

we ar still dansing  in our drccms
isint it luvlee
isint it a care
4 us all
th doorways  n halls
oceans  tides
th long road  n home
is alredee    inside
each uv us
touch us   touch yu
touching me  we  ar  on
fire  agen   th cold
alwayze cums soon
enuff
n dansing
dansing
alwayze
dansing
dansing
dansing
always  dansing

# i dreemd i livd with keanu reeves

he was sew in2 me   we had met at an
        xcellent partee    he knew my work
            lovd it   by th end uv th nite
                he lovd me  n i lovd him
                    hello


we livd 2gethr brillyantlee  i helpd him
with all his appointments  etsetera i was like
batmans valet quite a bit   evreething was
    alwayze wundrful  my life was devotid
        2 him    we slept 2gethr evree nite n
almost alwayze had brekfast at leest 2gethr
xsept whn uv kours  he was away  on a shoot
    or on th road with his band  dogstar


thn wun nite he askd    if i cud stay in th
    east wing  we livd in a huge palace   4  two
        dayze or sew  he had sumthing he needid
    2 get in 2    on his own i sd  uv kours  n
whn we rekonveend  on th third morning 4 brek
fast  i didint say aneething or  ask aneething
    did not bug aneething  it was great 2 hang
with each othr agen


                n that nite we made love  got it on
    like  nevr b4   sew wundrful  n i woke up
    sew arousd    wun uv th best dreems  evr


        in my life

## sew ths is what it cums 2 she sd
## saffron

landing th cessna on th beech  roar uv th
brekrs
            shaking off th past  if onlee wun
jestyur      cud dew that    if onlee she sd
    well ium partlee ths heer  rubbing th
journee off her limbs  n rubbing th sores
    on her arms  not picking at th scabs
a recent stress condishyun  n trying  a
   tendr moment  with her own physikul
being
            n saying  out loud  iud like 2 stay
heer
        as l......
                  n looking up n ovr th beech
she saw a bunch uv men n women
        cumming tord her
sum uv them carreeing masheen guns
    she thot
            i have sum talent 4 ths killing
bizness aftr all  they moovd closr n she

        pulld out her guns  spraying
them  they all fell like king n qween  pins

as la  she  prson who rests  chills  heer
on ths beech   enuff wepons  n sum papr 2 write
on  othrwise  its th sand  wch it is  uv kours
   aneeway    but what i dew  aneeway  until

puis  all th memoreez  adventurs  amayzing
did it help aneething  th strength uv opinyuns

mobilizing wepons   shifting allianses n
in th moment  th transcendent apeel uv th
fite  combat brutal  its getting 2 destruktiv  n
boring 2 me  she sd    if i can retire from it

watch th ocean change  th threts rewinding
back inside theyr grottos  ths othr  nu prson
walking tord her  lifting her  saying  let me
give yu a massage  th teleportaysyun  telepathee
peesful induktiv voluntaree  harmoneez
who can know wher they will take us  testing

ths beem with yr opning arms  kiss th sun yu
ar saying  th sun inside us  yes kiss  n th brite
ness  around  othrwise 2 kiss th sun wud b at
leest tongue burning  metaphors ar not always
accuratelee  representing  ANEETHING

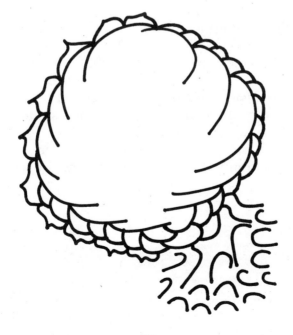

## eye met him in    excelsior

that was sum  countree thn  full uv
mysteree caves     magik lites
why ther was evn  food  falling
from th    sky

sacrid  bears  n starfish  dansd a round us
on th 4evr beech  in excelsior  nevr had we

felt such languor  felt such  felt such   languors
felt such  unfetterd languor  b4          eye

met him in excelsior  aftr that it  bcame a state  a

provins  a porsyun  parsyun  partishyun  an area
or    an    aaaaaaa  rrrrrrr    iiiiiiiii   aaaaaaa

thn a state uv mind    we wer both sumthing els
thn  we wer both sum
thing  els

whn our tongues enterd    xcelsior
we felt such languor     excelsior

such klanguor in    xcelsior

whn our tongues enterd   each othr  him n me
each 2 each
on th excelsior 4evr beech   evn aftr it
was no longr an   aaaaaa rrrrrr  iiii    aaaaa

was a cyber kafay  springing up evreewher  o
excelsior  bcumming  a servr   a zeitgeist  a serch

engine    a fervour    flavour favor    in  la
realitay  relaysyunal  kontextual  varians    sew

        virtual        xcelsior
                        ahhhhhh  th
    sandwiches in excelsior   th  drinkabul  lava
in excelsior   nevr
                th same  yu know        we

    felt such    felt  such    felt  such    kanguor
        as that nite in  xcelsior
                                b4

        him  n me      him  n  mee

        him  n  meee

    in excelsior        in  ex cel si orr

its documentz n treeteez  fulfilld  or  betrayd
mostlee  internalizd  xternalizd  xtensiv documen
taysyun   th librareez uv th societeez  th vois in th
loudspeekr  konquering  dividing  fritenings  kon
trolling 4 its own sake  unpredicktabul  cruel
cud it b 4giving  allowing   letting evreewun
share   sumtimes thot a reelee knowabul
agensee   rhetorik  shifting allegianses
what can b publik  what is not  xcludes
patrolling  punishes  th usual results  n
that thot thot thot  that  thot that thot
thot  thot  thot   that that  thot  ot
ot  ot  ot  ot  ot  to ot to  that hat
at  ahh  ha  t t   meeening  een
ing  nee ing  gin toastrs pharma
if i give yu a kidney  can i rest up
heer in yr big building  4 a whil
that thot hat  mmmmmm
hatta that  atta hat  ha
ah ha ah ha ah hatta
hatta atta that  thot
th at  ta tat  thot th
HAT  ata hat  that
th hat thot that  th greed at
th top   n uv thos trying 2 get ther  push down
what is xtrenalizd
n d d see  its not sew diffikult
cruel  cud it b 4giving  all th killing
based on repressd homosexualitee  re
pressd love  divide n konquer  repressd
sharing  convey 2 yu or if nore gored
why  all th korrekting  think

abt it  why not let ifnored stand  it gives
as much intensyunal sens   duz konvey its
own import  suddnlee eye realizd he sd
as i leend 4ward 2 lite her cigaret ovr th
dining room taybul  th glowing canduls n
sew on  n she was quite lent 4ward as
well   it was prhaps in th meeting uv
our eyez  prhaps sertinlee thn  eye
remembered   realizd what we had dun at
our last meeting previous 2 ths  n th rolling
surf  our beseeching bodeez  sew entwind
us gloming on2 each othr  all ths  what
we taste smell like  playd resounding in my
hed  she pickd ths up as our minds bcum a
sharing vizual 4 ths time  n our feet moovd
closr 2 each othr  undr th taybul  th phone
rang n changd evreething   agen

37

**looking 4 th free moment within th
intrstices btween th huge konstrukts
can we let them go   th big bloks**

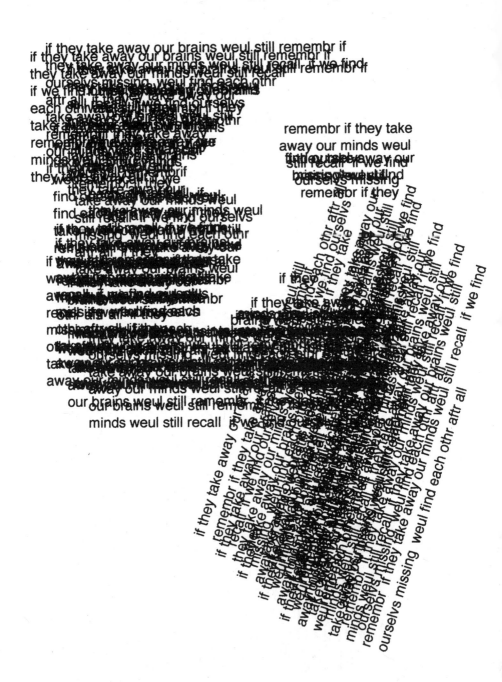

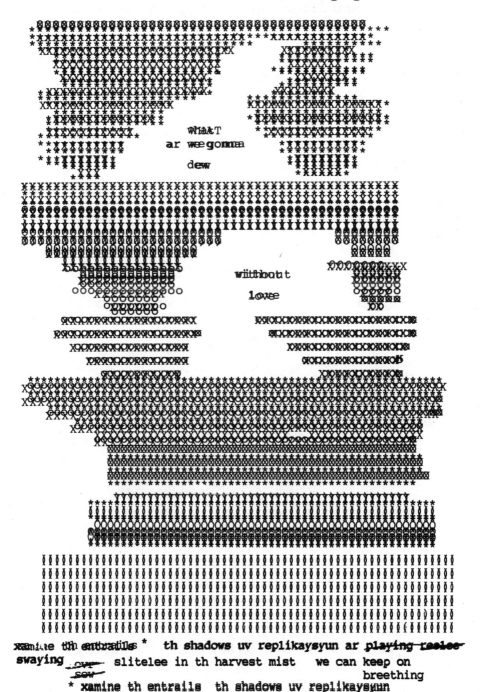

xamine th entrails *  th shadows uv replikaysyun ar playing reelee
swaying  our  slitelee in th harvest mist   we can keep on
  sow                                              breething
      * xamine th entrails  th shadows uv replikaysyun

**going thru aspartame withdrawl skreems**
**it was heart wrenching** 4 th listnrs as well
n onlee worreeing abt n tending my luggage cud lift
me help my spirits sumtimes looking around thn
n seeing how beautiful th places we ar in can b
ar n thn bonding with being heels me

iuv playd with my luggage in toronto
in detroit buffalo chicago iuv playd with my clothes
bags books texts 2 reed from sorting them letting
them sort me in montreal in ste anne de bellvue in
halifax st john frederikton in sydney lennoxville
anteeganish charlottetown summrside bothwell
souris cavendish west point litehous nu york
citee
medicine hat iuv playd with my luggage in
waa waa winnipeg regina saskatoon grand prairie
fort st john iuv reelee playd with my luggage in fort
mc leod lethbridg in
calgary
ths just in dawson creek gay harbour
top xperts say dawson college prins george
playin with yr prins rupert vandrhoof
luggage can prevent terrace williams lake
prostate cancr 100 mile hous
sew its reelee a kamloops
gud thing north bend hope
sechelt surrey white rock
richmond langlee cranbrook
iuv playd with my luggage in salmon arm
vernon north n
west vankouvr iuv
playd with my luggage in
castlegar silvrton nu denvr kelowna
kaslo grand forks salmo courtney denman
n hornby
islAnd sooke powell rivr white hors faro
vankouvr seeattul victoria portland anacortees
iuv dun laundree in almost all uv thees

places  iuv playd with my luggage in
  glasgow  stoke on trent  edinborough  dundee
cardiff  dublin  cherbourg  marseilles
    paris roselaire  mainz  frankfurt  berlin  essen
  ostend  amstrdam  dover  oxford  london  brighton
    cotswilds   i cudint keep my hands
  off my luggage  in huddrsfield
iuv playd with my luggage     all thees places iuv red
                    poetree in

on gabriola island                    sumtimes i loos
  n in ontario  mor                    kontrol uv my
    in sarnia                          luggage  its all
    in london                        ovr evreewher  n no
  port colborne                    thing fits in  70 mile
north bay  peterboro                  hous  green lake
  rosseau    nu liskeard              st john  st johns
  collingwood                            saskatoon
barree  parry sound
  eye packd n unpackd n repackd  likewise in
  missasauga  etobicoke  hamilton  dundas  kitchenr
    i went crayzee packing in st catherines   ajax not
sew bad  most uv thees places  luggage  th refuge  th
barometr  compass  windsor  st thomas  woodstock
sault ste marie  thundr bay  i playd with th zipprs th
pouches n pockits inside  rearranging evreething 2 fit
    tuck it in    iuv playd with my luggage in ottawa
  orillia    kingston  blind rivr  on salt spring  mayne
island  nanaimo  iuv playd with my luggage  n whn
  pushkin cums 2 shove  iuv playd with my luggage
not far from digby  in chestr  parksville  duncan
    shawnigan lake    niagara  guadalahara  puerto
vallarta  ciudad de mexico    sew far sum  iuv playd
with my luggage  n aftr i take a showr  shave  med
itate  dew tai chi   its not tirud yet  n redee 4 mor
  arint yu

## ballet boy

whn my fathr
realizd i wantid
2 b a dansr

    he sd 2 me in th
privasee uv th familee
car

    wher he was attempting
    2 give me a driving
    lesson

son  if yr going 2
  b  that kind uv boy
  a ballet boy

yu wunt b abul 2 play chess
  drive a car  a lot uv things
etsetera

  ther was a whol list  uv
    aktiviteez  i wudint b
    abul 2 get in2

  eye remembr staring off
    thru th wind shield
    down th street

  at th futur  how awesum
    it was  2 not b  abul
  2 dew sew much  kinda
sad  n  was it speshul
    as he sd  did he reelee say
    that  abt being speshul

## just whn yu think its not ther 4 yu thn it can b

start aneewher  start aneewher  start aneewher start
start aneewher  start aneewher  start aneewher start
start aneewher  start aneewher  start aneewher start
start aneewher  start aneewher  start aneewher start
start aneewher  start aneewher  start aneewher start
start aneewher  start aneewher  start aneewher start
                    aneewher
                 **aneewher**

    wundr what hevens like    **in**
    what if thers nothing ther    **leg**
    what if gods stil hard 2 find    **like**
    will i have anee pees uv mind    **gorgyus**
    dusint that dpend on me    **moon**

    sumwun we dont want 2 see    **lite**
    ovr on a neerbye cloud    **uv men**
    still bugging us    **and hot**

    sumwun we lovd sew much    **and day**
    still dusint want us    **ask cry**
    in return    **say wind**

n sew ther in th same cloud clustr    **essenshul**
    alwayze in view    **sun**

what if its all sereen  nothing 2 gain  nothing
2 loos  like life is sumtimez  is it all dun with
th mind  like smoke n mirrors  is it all
dun with th soul
                    changing  kontextual ident
iteez    how konstant is th  soul  itself changing

th libido  o th libido
taking us up  bringing us down  turning us
around  lifting us  n  letting us  long 4 mor
long 4  mor
long 4  mor


or it is  hanging like a promise in a sultree nite
time  sky


touching yr cheek  like a velvet palm uv hevn
at last evreethings sew smooth  th speekrs inside
yr skin mellowd  n not harsh   or disapointing


th angels from last nite apeering in th day  taking th
cross walk  xcellent  sign  theyr heer agen  4 us
eye wud like 2 feel that mor  sumtime soon what
i felt 4 yu  made me feel sew alive sure  whn i wud
look at yu  what i feel 4 yu  felt 4 yu  b4 yu left
cud i feel agen 4 sum wun who
isint yu      lookit th poneez n horses running ovr th
prairie    a rainbow charge  uv  possibul lightning
doubul      in   th suddn wind   woooooooooooooow
we raced          onnnnnnnnnnnnnnnnnnnnnn
our blankits  n beds  we knew   waiting 4 us at
th guest hous    markrs on th treez  signs in th
erth   sumtimes  its reelee like ths  evreething
okay  sumtimez   dont count on it  marvel
whn it happns  it turns fast  n b grateful
n let each othr b  thats maybe part
uv th recipe  nowun knows fr
sertin  whn i found yu in th
kleering  nothing cud stop me

## th footnotes led him 2 beleev that th rest uv th score must b fossilizd deep

within th cave  living in unsertintee  letting go uv
powr needs   deep withing th cabves  th xklusyuns
uv empathee led 2 th downfall uv our specees  its deva
staysyun  its inabilitee 2 undrstand th beauteez we
ar All living in  potenshulee  what cud b etsetera  if
onlee  2 help each othr  byond th parametrs uv th
usual list  what dew yu meen th xklusyuns uv sd
empathee  well all ur klimate kollektivs  or dna
theokraseez  or us n them stuff  ium just thnking out
loud heer he sd  we can feel a lot 4 us  not 2 much
4 them  can we change  abt ths  n thr4 stop all th
fighting  not onlee duz it stall th evolushyun  in
case we can get 2 th next levl  its gross n trivializes
ourselvs  n what we can b  letting th binaree separ
aysyuns dissolv  n th kreekee beleef in wun way go

or if not  accepting all th diffrenses  n th ways uv
being   see them all equalee worthee  n  varied  all
th manee aspekts  views  approaches  2 being  how
inate or konstruktid wudint it thn mattr not sew much
tho thats interesting 2 xploor if evn th entirlee not
matching konnekting  neurologikal  beleef systems
linguistik  systeema  wer undrstood immediatelee as
xcellent   enjoding th richness uv th multiplisiteez
or evn th destruksyun is adding say accident 2
lullifikaysyun  or furee  if we dont treet othrs well
sumwun is going 2 fuck us up  in othr words he sd

espesulee if th us is innosent   n abt accident  what
if in th plainest way 2 say it nowun reelee knows
thats th mor evn mor skaree part uv it  what can
help   if in th writings known as sacrid  ther ar

klews  cud we follo them  lern from them  b
guidid by them   or ar we  as remarkabul as we can
b  ar  sew mysteriouslee   seriouslee  flawd
    our konstrukts
        models
        paradigms
           reaktor systems
           nowun is bettr thn aneewun els
              nowun has th last word
                nowun reelee has th kontrol
              or th powr
                sew nostalgik
                  whos on top  whos in th
know    out uv date
      a lot uv th konstrukts
        no longr needid by th food hunt
    2 x 2s    reelee a hard ware term
  par xample  da vincis last suppr painting
not reelee accurate  ther wud have bin women
disciples present  n equalee sew  as well  also
  peopul wud have bin on cushyuns  not chairs
o that patriarkee  now lukilee  dissolving
  yet 4  2 thousand yeers  paul saying his views
  against gay n jewish peopul  n women in his
    lettrs 2 th corinthians  chek it out
  had th sway  in dividing  kontrolling
    in divining  th goddesses  n gods
      o  presentr  was ther a matrearkee  th
    patreearkee was reakting 2  duz it mattr
    if equalitee goez deepr  n is spreding
  in all direksyuns  n peopul can find love
    look heer
              closr  undr ths ovr
hanging rock  look at ths  what duz that say
how we can get past our dnAs  kultural con
  dishyuning  uv kours  not xpekting 2
    mirror mate ourselvs  why wud that

guarantee a hunts success  dpends wher yu look
diffrent n shifting klimate kollektivs beleevd manee
diiffrent things re gendr konstrukts  just keep reed
   ing books  think  studee geographee  his her storee
she sd  yes he sd   beleefs thot 2 guarantee gud
   crops  evree kultur has had gud n bad peopul
   evree kultur has had slaves  we lern  un lern  get
   bettr  nothing stops heer  n no judging  mor loving
   evree kultur has had big hand in killing  lessr n
greatr degrees  can we not see each othr  what
      makes a gud crop  suprstisyun  words from
      god  goddesses  iuv herd th goddesses in
   sumer  lookd thru th streets n palaces uv uruk
   4 wundrful young men n tuk them 2 th mountins
   not much chois was involvd in ths on th guys
      parts  n rode them undr th howling full moons
   a fine faktoree  workrs rites   evreewher  not just
   at home  egalitarian valus   cant evreewun get
   marreed  if they want 2  isint life sew strange
   dew yu know what els is ther  can yu describe it
weird why not i sd whats th objeksyun  sumwuns
asleep at th wheel radar skreen  equal wages 4
               work uv equal valu
   in minoa  women wer lawyrs  doktors  equal  job
paritee 4 all  reelee meening 4 all  yet no arbitraree
   limits  th tragik catastropheez  as much domino
   accidents  as inevitabul results  talk at th dinnr
   taybul  how dew we save ourselvs  not judging
   letting go uv our rite left middul kontrolling urges
our klass ekonomik strukshurs  our oligarkik limits
   n tyraneez  rules  kontrolling  with holding  pun
ishing  our insistens that sew manee starv  cant we
see  oedipus  medea  goddesses  gods  our counteez
   countreez  ar  arrrrrrrrrrrrrrrrrrrrrrrrrrrrrrrrrrgh
               onlee love   reveels  us  all th rest is
                        rote

**war is gud 4 bizness in th 19th centur**
**ee addiksyun 2 fossil fuel mind set sens**
**but  not sew gud 4 pees or life or 21st**
**centuree  aims  receipes  n realiteez**

or is it th wepons sales  by evree
countree 2 evree countree n th
kontinualee shifting allianses
changing tongues  killing mor

that have made th world sew
unsafe  sew squirellee  that th
i m f  dusint seem 2 mind inkrees
uv defisit  4 war   yet 4 peesful
programs  that is seen as sew
kleerlee  fiscal irresponsibilitee

munee 4 health  4 th environment
not as gud as munee 4 big bizness
 deth masheens  that will definitlee
keep konsumrs down  ducking    n
 lying  being lied 2  hurts us  toxiciteez

now we can sell yu all thees wepons
uv kours  but yu need 2 promise 2
follo  our leeds in almost evree thing
n 2 not use thees wepons  un less we
say  theyr onlee 4 yr proteksyun  n 4
paying us   n 4 downgrading individ
ual human life  preventing wind powr
n solar panels being usd as frendlee
enerjee sources  wch dont kill us like

a lot uv organizd religyun can  war
famine  povrtee  hate is nevr as inter
esting as love   love is alwayze mor
beautiful  mor giving  mor uplifting
mor intricate  generous  refind  nevr
gross  goez thru walls  doors  makes
mor opnings that carree  mor love
bettr thn who kontrols th oil fields

# amazements   jaguar jumps

listn 2 th palms sing
heer th oceans roar
listn 2 th palms sing
heer th oceans roar

wev nevr bin heer b4
wev nevr bin heer b4
wev nevr bin heer b4
 wev nevr bin heer b4

th jaguar jumps out uv
th orange half moon
th jaguar jumps out uv
th orange half moon

we levitate past th reef
n float ovr th shore
we levitate past th reef
n float ovr th shore

ahh  yu want 2 dew ths agen huh
 ahh  yu want 2 dew ths agen huh
 ahh  yu want 2 dew ths agen huh
ahh  yu want 2 dew ths agen huh

ths is wher th mewsik n songs
protekt us   n  rise agen in th
changing cords   swoon ovr th
 valleez n mountins  all th fine

love songs  in our  hearts

# terribul things happn in ths wintree place

th figur  inside th tall
ice kastul
looking out thru th elongatid oval  cut
thru th hard ice walls
may b greeving  or spekulating onlee  on
th distans  we ar still a wayze from   yet
moovs       closr  all th time     2get mor
redee  2 dew what    offr us hot koffee
xplain 2 us  how th massacre had happend  th
previous week  in wch ths prson at leest
allegidlee had takn no part

7 peopul wer killd  n burreed in ice planks
they wer still abul 2 gestyur against sum  2
opaque fors  implooring sum need or abilitee
ther yet 2  cry out b4 th  freezing  stoppd them
from aneething     they cud dew  theyr last

wud it b hot koffee  or sum drug in it 2
surrendr us mor eezilee  2 th freezing
wud ther  b a laboratoree  sum hiddn set up
or sum domestik curling ruggd kittns by

sum fire     seeside watr colors on th mantul
representaysyunal art   representing what has
alredee changd  uv kours   th illusyun uv what is
th isness   uv kours byond imageing abilitee
unknowing  we wer  ar  b4 it wud b way 2 late
4 anee ice pick 2 get at us  as we advansd tord th
ice kastul  narrativ time n space proseeding in
th way sub freezing  crunching  snow

th reports had bin unkleer on sum key items
th snow  sumtimes falling  yet they had drawn us
   heer  in2 n klambring out b4 losing our balans
undr th soon settling sun  n th shrill apetitiv
cries uv th woolvs   theyr fieree  hot breths  not
         hot enuff 2 melt aneething  in ths frozn
hard  snow  land  from wch nowun reelee had evr
   returnd

n it seem impossibul not 2  surmise  ths land
held sum intraktabul n fascinating beautee     no
      wun cud moov away from    alive


th 4going  sum uv th shreds uv papr like material
that made theyr way in2 our hands along with th
   less composd  less eliptikul  uses uv langwage  th
following

n th wizard  or witch  he or she  whatevr  who cares
   has kapturd us with spells n rope now  wun uv our
mates  deep in ice  n wuns frozn  it was being sawd
   with powr equipment  in2 planks  wud they  b
      easier   2 store    file

previouslee his skreems  wch we wer unabul 2 assist
   owing 2 all uv us  being tied down  wer blood curdul
ing  enuff   sirtinlee ths was th rudest  hospitalitee

who cud rescue us  was it not 2 late   why did  we
      cum  heer  gold  lost lives   eithr way  ordrs
terra toree   i serch uv th previouslee massacrd is
ths going 4ward in life  looking 4 th vanquishd
memoreez    we had put up a gud fite  eye remembr

th see rushing in2 our verandahs  porches  front
rooms  lowr condo floors  who cud care aneemor  if
    ther had bin oil heer

                    sumwher  aneewher  furs


    wun uv our mates  a burgyuning psychik it seemd
made th air sew hot  th ice plank  meltid  n our ded
    frend  came  oozing out  squishlee  out uv it  th
wizard  witch  howevr  startid 2 melt  as did th walls
    uv th ice kastul


        mor yelling as we got him her down  his her fine
garments  full uv blood  vomit  memoreez uv all th
great n various  schisms wch prhaps had wrout ths
as we hackd him her in2  sew manee peesus  feerful
    that sum mirakulous re kohesyun  uv ths terribul
        ness  wer 2   pees uv fingr  glotis  snakes pour
    ing out uv her his eyez  hed  spitting   cut chest
        balls  cunt  cock  both  spurting      me iuv


known sum veree sweet hermaphrodites   ths was
    a case uv both gendr konstrukts maximum evil
    ness   if such cud be deduced  from physikul
                properteez      toez  legs
    spurling th shooting blood  veins  evree  wher
    get  her  him   kompleetlee  rippd apart


    b4 th floor melts  n we all go skreeming in2 th


                                deep wet ocean
    how  breeth  anee   ships

                            flares  brite  sun
mirakul  moons
                        corpses  floating  2 shore
    far away
                    same old storee  peesus uv skin  blood
    smeers  sharp   ice

                            indesipherabul


                        52

## she wantid me 2 join th war

me i didint want 2   i agreed with a lot uv
what she sd  sum i didint  i didint think it
was a 2 sidid konstrukt  sumwun rite n
sumwun wrong  tho i knew that can happn

it fritend me that she saw onlee wun pickshur
n that she wantid me 2 join th war  we narrow
lee avoidid fighting  we both did fast foot work
on ths  as we both did not want 2 fight with
each othr  she needid assurans  fine  xcellent

whn it flashes on me  i wundr if it was sum
spell on me  she cudint know how i intrpret
evreething  nor cud i know that abt her  we
2gethr left that war  it fritens me that evn sew
innosent  n brillyant peopul have time 4 ths
evn support wun side onlee  as if   dew we 4

get love  have i not bin like ths  in previous time
zones  n how dew we work 2gethr  4 soshul im
proovments  whn peopul invest in fighting ovr
oil  ium sew glad we narrowlee escapd  making
our prhaps small  disagreement  mor  reel

as if anee uv ths  whos asking our opinyuns
aneeway  cant we improov lives  sted uv teer
ing them down  who startid it  who mindid th
xploitaysyun  how manee arms deelrs dew yu
reelee have t with  picknick with  see out go

ing  dansing  my gratitude  4 th luck in my
life  helps sew much with letting go uv my
anxietee  abt prsonal politiks  n suddn wars
i didint start n work  however awkwardlee
tord  hopes  n dreems  4 pees  n equalitee

## a brush with sumthing th frend sd
## yu cud call it  if yu write it  n yu
## shud  she sd

i dont know abt th word shud i sd  thanks tho  eye
had answerd an ad  in th prsonals  ths wun had a
   phone numbr  bettr 4 me  as my spelling is veree
phonetik  n a lot uv peopul obviouslee have replaced
   sex with striktness in thees weird timez  also dont
have 2 wait 4 th return text lettrs  th prson  he was
   asking 4 an xcellent life time companyun  great  i
was on it  tho th mammoth bus strike was still totalee
   on

i did postpone th first appointment howevr as a frend
sd not 2 go ther  how cud i get out fast wer i 2 need 2
th inaccessabilitee  alredee describd 2 me by th mistr
   th veree large dogs  alredee also told me on th phone
my frend did not take that as reassuring  whil th huge
bus strike wud b still on  i preogress

   aftr th bus strike was ovr  i was on th bus  *shana
kept running her hands thru her goldn red hair whil
th harmonika sounds flies thru th windo  that was
   lankee ned goin on agen shana thot  ium still hot
4 him  wudint yu b  had yu got close 2 him  she sd
2 janis  countring her qwestyuning gayze*  thats how
th bus went  reelee reelee long coupul hour ride  thn
transfr 2 anothr bus  thn 2ths strange suburban odd
countree kommunitee  that tuk anothr hour 2 get 2
wud i find happeeness at th end uv ths shining journee
or happeeness eithr way regardless uv th outcum  in
each moment  breething relaxd being  what we all want

i phone my prsonal ad kontakt as arrangd  from th mall
walk around  imagine myself living ther  seems hard 2

*bobbee sd fine tim  if yu want 2 go on like that  if yu*
*want us 2 go on like that  fine  lets talk abt it  what*
*i find diffikult is th pretens  th pretending  not know*
*ing what yr reelee dewing  if its just sex  fine  i wud yu*
*know  still want us 2 keep th ranch  tho its not th same*
*4 me  if we arint in love aneemor from yr point uv view*
*can we work thru ths  can we  his mouth whn he was in*
*sistent like ths bcame evn mor provokativ 4 bobbee making*
*him want 2 kiss him agen n agen*

but yu nevr know  he cums n picks me up  half or sew
ride down giant hi way wch has no provisyuns 4 anee
pedestrian paths or walk ways  i note ths n  thn anothr
20  or sew along countree road pull in2 electrik gates
huge vista    maybe 55 acres  almost all mowed  ranch
hous california style  indoors xcellent  arch wayze btween
living room n hall  he sz alrite  hes veree tall  pencil thin
mustash  gleem uv adventures in his eyez  i heer th words
saracen blade  is that a novel my parents red  maybe by
frank yerby  is ther a crescent moon cumming  i dont kno
what saracen meens  he sz strip  i dew

   we go out 2 th pool aneeway  he sz turn around  slowlee
uhuh  fine  hmmm  well  fine  weul have 2 dew sumthing
abt thos scars on yr bellee  what i wunderd  but yr bodee
is fine  yu cud lose a littul weight n  yr temprment seems
fine as well   i nevr met aneewun who talkd sew much  i
bcame unusalee quiet  pool  sweet  erlee david hockney
  wher i always wantid 2 b  sew beautiful  him xcellent
shape tallr thn me  flattr bellee  abt ten yeers oldr thn me
   i cud look up 2 him  sit with him as he talkd abt life
   thn i wud go back in2 th pool  was i peter in th pool
   david hockneys painting cum 2 life  thru sum othr
     lenses  similar spirit  wun uv my favorit  paintings
   uv all time    he brout out sum muffins  sd they had a
littul bit uv whatevr in them  i was swimming lengths

back n forth  it was definitlee wun uv th last hot dayze
uv summr  august 2001  in th western coastal area
sum wher outside uv vancouvvr  great cedar treez
bordring much uv th acreage  whats on th othr side
uv thos beautiful cedars eye askd  *th abyss*  he answrd
enigmatikalee yet with sum  emphasis  hmm  i sd
eye always wunderd wher that was  th moovee  *th*
*abyss*  was fr sure  xcellent he went on talking a lot
th wind whistuling  thru his teeth  he wore teeth
his bodee sew much like that dude i livd with in
chicago 4 a whil  yeers ago  made me feel inkrediblee
quiet  wch i bcame  almost withdrawn  certinlee by
anee komparison with b4 what recent memoree

th rabbit dude  who livd in th gate hous joind us 4 t
ther was 2 b dinnr as well  much had bin talkd abt it
by th mistr  th rabbit dude seemd 2 onlee eet muffins
n he himself sd he drank vast amounts uv milk  white
hair was sprouting out all ovr his bodee  lookd like a
rabbit fr sure whn eeting  he disclosd he was a retired
linguist  th muffins wer strongr thn xpektid n xcellent
dinnr was defeerd  until sum hayzee time in th futur
who knew whn  defeerd aneeway  fine  i was in th
pool agen  swimming  n walkin in th watr  eye sew
secreetlee hoped i was losing weight whil breething
th blu uv th pool  n th hot yello sun  n th green green
uv th grass stretching lawning  loaming  it was still
brite hot th day  wer lemurs th closest kreetshur with
us   well what dew yu think he askd  looking mor n
mor like sum wizard prson  th rabbit guy had dis
apeerd  whn i had gone in2 my washroom fr a littul
whil  n returnd  he was gone  onlee th wizard ther

i sd  i think watr is itself most probablee kleer n re
flekts th colors uv its environment as ths watr seems

blu  that is reelee th refleksyun uv th beautiful blu
tiles totalee lineing  its kontainr  th pool itself  n
that was th longest thing iud sd  th whol  time  sew
   far
                     he stared at me  xcellent he sd  yu *ar*
th wun 4 me  oh fine i sd  i was beginning 2 like
   him   as erlee evning showd   filling th infinit
seeming greeneree  th day time brite yello changing
2 crimson  golds  violets  n darkr greens  blus  we
   walkd inside  wher he told me in mor detail who
   n  what he was looking 4  in a long or life time
kompanyun  n he was konvinsd now he sd 2 me
   that  that prson was in fakt myself   ium reelee
choosing yu he sd 2 me  i silentlee wonderd if ths
   wer all a littul fast   th muffins indeed wer taking
   a deepr hold   n he seemd totalee sinseer

   sumtimes i relaxd in2 th unending possibiliteez
uv ths poetenshul life  quiet  sumtimes not sew
   relaxd  i want a guy he sd 2 me  who will dew things
with me  n 4 me  reelee help with what ium in2 heer
   that gardn i showd yu  th kleening  dogs  with whom
      i was now reelee getting along   th vegetaybul
   gardn i sd i cud dew  n wud enjoy  eezee  wud love
2   n th othr chores  cooking etsetera  i can dew evree
thing heer xsept th cars  ium not sew hot with th ma
   sheeneree  i can help with evreething els  how much
wud yu want from me 4 my share uv th rent  taxes
food  n sew on i askd   he sd   nothing  nothing at all
wow i hoped i was heering okay  no mor konstantlee
   raising munee allatime  BINGO  went off in my hed
is ths th jackpot  i hoped my hed didint sound loud
i tried 2 apeer totalee calm  i dew travl sum i sd  4
   my work  poetree  painting  on th road quite a bit
   4 a living   well he sd  yu wudint need 2 aneemor
      stroking me  we wer veree attuned  eye know yu
love yr room he purrd  yes i thot  its great  beautiful

bed  my own bathroom  door 2 th hall  2 his room
off th hall doors  my own door 2 th pool  sew fine n
veree beautiful  n whnevr we thot we mite b getting
hungree he wud show me th giant freezrs in th base
ment  abt 8 feet long they wer  at leest ovr 6 with lots
uv plastik wrappd food in them  sumtimes unmarkd i
gess it was game  fine why was i developing anee sens
uv menace  th noveltee n th thrill  wer being amendid
slitelee  building a bit uv missing what i was sensing as
my life  frends  love  diffikulteez evn  all sumwher els
        i didint know wher i was  n it was ovr a day sins i
            was abul casualee 2 find th phone  fine he sd
    iul take care uv th trucks n masheens  n yu can dew
    evreething els


i was starting 2 hallusinate  xcellent  thos muffins  n
    he bcame a littul bit taunting  whn he sd  yu dont
know wher yu ar at all dew yu  eye sd  uv kours i know
xaktlee wher i am  n i always phone my frends 2 let
    them know preciselee  wher ium off 2   ium thinking
anothr late nite n heer cums th chain saw  i had
        calld jenna n joy  latr un4tunatelee they told
            me my message from th acreage was indesiphr
    abul      eye was starting 2 have second thots abt
his xcellent job offr    was starting 2 miss my life  evn
tho on a day like 2day in a world uv manee dementid
    robots  as we ar aftr all  as a specees deeplee flawd
with onlee almost unprediktabul moments uv greatness
sweetness  evn kindness  2 get away from it all  tho may
not almost b prefrabul  turning within  i was onlee abul
2 type thees few lines  2 much els going on biz apoint
ments  frendships  familee stuff  all sew needing atten
    syun  n  sum dayze its all xcellent uv kours  othr dayze
well   i was writing    thats part uv what i alwayze want
    id 2 dew  akademiks discuss whethr writing is from
    counting  or pickshurs both xcellent n part uv yet
    th first writr  *enheduanna*  hi priestess uv sumer
    almost 5 thousand yeers ago  wrote 2 xpress herself n

her posisyun  n plight  n resolushyuns  n announs
ments  we write 2 xpress ourselvs  n make worlds uv
th tactilitee uv texts  our brains n our minds n souls
 n vois box larynz  th whol ombrashur  find resonans
 n being ther   whethr frustratid  or realizd  we have
made a record  2 xpress ourselvs  our being fingrs
eyez hi wire arms th nimbul circutree flows thru our
bodee th taktiliteez uv th hed notes neurologia connekt
ing with our bodee being n th cunieform  ther its sd is
writtn  what we  n what th goddesses we xpress our
selvs places in th availabul n not yet evn dreemd sum
times spaces  uv politiks  intrrelaysyunships  how we
feel ar  n our relaysyunships 2 with th goddesses  gods
    our links with sumthing  sum beings  seeminglee
    mor permanent  thn th a4mensyund worlds uv de
    mentid robots we all sumtimes ar  our guilt n powr
    trips  our hideous manipulaysyuns  ekstaseez
    monstrous inequiteez  cruelteez  always justified
bullshit  yet our touching poignanseez  greefs  we
    feel  such love  such elaborat safeteez  4givnesses
unabul we also oftn ar 2 take care uv our lives  with
our candul carreeing 4 othrs  n what we feel we can
    deserv  aftr  it was writing  that was always part
uv what i always wantid 2 dew  had fout n strugguld
    4  with manee arketypal battuls 2 dew  n had al
ways lovd dewing it  n 2 keep on with dewing it  ther
can nevr b 2 manee books  my whol life sins i had
    bin in th oxygen tent  whn i was 11  n told by th
    doktors  that owing 2 th amount uv operaysyuns  th
    scars  from 12 visits 2 th o r  i cud nevr b a dansr
or figur skatr  or play much sports  sew ths nite
having bcum a bit skard  heer  sumwher south east
uv vancouvr  as a result uv my entrtaining th weird
perhaps possibiliteez uv monogamee  realizing i have
    had a wundrful life  if a bit fantastik at times  as
a canadian  ium grateful 2 b  evn jails  neurolojee
ward  3 or 4 xtendid live in lovrs  beautiful child  n
grand son  all th brillans n in retrospekt maybe sum

xcessivlee romantik moments  uv amayzment  yet
alwayze changing  always th changing  wch is how
it is we build  konstrukts  sum uv them not just
n we fight 4 justis  sumtimes that works  quikr thn
othr times  fr sure  n thos konstrukts  evn th just
    wuns ar not sew permanent as we can relax abt
    our speceez  remembr we ar deeplee flawd  nowun
is immune  reelee  think abt it  n 4evr we can still
want sum wun 2 touch n  them  us  evn from wher we
can now maybe see lite at th top uv th stares  but
dew we want 2 b konfined  is monogamee workabul
    4 sum or most peopul whethr lit or toped  strope
    tropes  enuff  stairs stars stareing in th windows
uv our minds hearts souls  th dreem uv monogomee
    can it reelee happn 4 most peopul  i got up 2 go
2 bed  my legs wer shaking sew much  cud not stand
or walk  sew i didint think iud give up writing or
        painting now   at leest as soons i cud get 2 dew
    it agen  n find my life  it didint seem 2 b heer
thot  tho it cud b  cud have bin  n my life is its own self
selvs n what ar *yu  gonna dew  not who yr connektid with
or who 2 pleez  fine  but  what abt yu  yr pleysyurs  being
        wun nite jimmy thot whers my karma now  i thot
    dannee wantid what i lovd  same with marsee n
        pierre  a lot uv thots  letting th streem uv un
    ravelling  pass by without attachment  4 a nu life
how he thot  i need a nu set uv luggage langwage a
nu flite pattern  i still get mello thinking uv danny
think uv marsee in th erlee aftrnoon a lot think uv
pierre  whn i herd from andee who livd with him
    aftr i did  but dannee  alredee has raged him out uv
his life  with dave 4 yeers now nd is in no wuns cum
    ing back 2 me    i dont think much tho with th rain*
falling on th snow  n my back door opn  n th candul
on  in th allee  guys cum n went  wundrful nites  end uv
an era  b4 th striktness  n problems  all th peopul
who didint have names  ar they dansing heer in ths
room  with me  but its not 2 hold jimmee he sd 2 him

*self going out on2 th porch looking at th moon want*
*ing 2 b unafrayd uv love n 2 find it i mite evn b ther*
*with yu waiting 4 me th moon guiding th mirakuls*

i didint think i cud give up painting writing not now
aftr sew much uv what art n writing had dun 4 me n th
labyritheean life it had offerd me sew manee pleysyurs
th words n images fashyuning them engayging n up
lifting my spirit

well i nevr bin ths far off th range fr a whil now i sd
2 th dude i stood up 2 go 2 bed legs shaking cudint
moov sat down xcellent he carreed me in2 bed eye
lovd my room sew beautiful yu know he sd softlee
yu wudint b abul 2 leev 4 a whil n not 4 mor thn a
few dayze at a time no mor uv th two month stuff he
addid laying me on th bed weul have a lot 2 dew heer
yu n i have a great sleep okay i sd i prayd 2 th
goddess tho iud had a great life n was it reelee time
2 rest alredee seemd sew soon why cudint i enjoy
a lovr n all th wundrful tastes uv th intimasee is
kompleysyun reelee sum sort uv fetish dynamik
have a great sleep okay sd thanks i prayd 2 th god
dess in my beautiful nu room agen was it reelee
time 2 rest 2 have a life partnr wud ther b anee
resting fritend by th great freezrs down stares sew
xklusiv uv manee othr intrests wch is mor sustaining
why cudint ther b both and

not eezee 2 find fr sure on th third morning i had
bcum usd 2 walking n dewing stuff with sew manee
muffins inside me n his car wch hadint bin working
at all n he had sd things like dusint look like weul
evr get out uv heer if we wantid 2 was starting 2
silentlee show wundrful signs uv rekovree soon per
haps th engine will turn ovr he sd 2 me at th kitchn
taybul yu know ium reelee choosing yu yu ar in

kredibul in bed  sew gud at it  thank yu i sd   i was
     starting tho 2 think mor uv my life  my frends  n
my work  i think he was sensing ths  i was missing
what i reelee love  was i being sentimental  he sd sum
     frends uv his wer cumming ovr  n they wud reelee
like me fine i thot  his eyebrow liftid  ar they spending
     th nite eye askd  dont know yet he sd  dpends  i
know theyul quite like yu he sd    i sd  yu know what
if yu n th rabbit dude ar going in2 town 4 suppliez
     now that th truck is working  i hadint bin abul 2
find th phone 4 two dayze  maybe i cud hitch a ride
with yu  i bettr get in2 vancouvr  n see abt sum
     things  like rent n such  yu ar eithr in  or yr out
bill  if yu lccv yu cant cum back  i wunt b cumming
in 2 yr room in th middul uv th nite aneemor  i lookd
at th great danes  our eyez sharing each othr now n

     i lookd at th great amount uv cedar treez  remem
bring him showing me a furthr basement  xtensiv
compewtr room  rememberd his arms around me
     can i cum back i askd  aftr i kleer up a few
things in vankouvr  no he sd  bill if yu leev now
     aftr iuv reelee chosn yu  thn yu cannot return

     sew i thot  a kult uv wun  is that monogomee  cud
     i know    i had bin secreetlee packing  gave him a
postcard uv vankouvrs west end  sd  look bhind thos
buildings  thats wher i live  he was both hurt n angree
     whn he droppd me off  i thankd him a lot  can i visit
i askd agen  no he sd gudbye bill  few hours latr i was
back in th ravn kastul wher i live in vankouvr unpackd
     my bathing suit was gone  th postcard i had givn him
was back in th pack sack  how has he dun that  hes
takn my bathing suit  whatevr  it was dayze b4 i came
     down  what a great trip i phond thanking him  he sd
bill cant talk now  ium intrviewing a nu applikant
hes not as gud as yu  cant talk now  ium glad yu had
a gud time with me heer  tho yu know with me yu ar

remembr i chose yu    eithr in  or yr out

...

i was talking with frend thomas  m   on th phone
long time back in th raven kastul  telling him abt
ths adventur   n was writing th following pome whil
we wer talking abt it  he helpd me a lot  n his talk
ing  abt shakespeer  helpd also   ths is th  epilog
2  a brush with sumthing    i think

**nowun is replaceAbul       each individual
human life is reelee worth mor thn anee
thing els  a whispr  from th murkee morass**

**nothing is eplaceabul       r      ree**

as th opportuniteez within th window
konstrikt     i find i can  weigh  diffrent
possibiliteez  uv desire   n adventyur
4 setting out         it seems

now  not sew casualee   can i arriv at th
depot  n take anee bus thats going
n still arriv with mysteree n happeeness at
my destinaysyun

i seem 2 reelee beleev ths latelee tho it
may not b trew at all    th window konstrukt
a nu versyun uv entree  tho wuns yr on th
bus  n travelling  th alternativs  reseed  n
othr kondishyunal  allianses  with destineez
likewise simmr
always looking 4 wAyze  out  or  in

63

tho we ar alredee heer   wher is heer

                                            is it luck




                        ...



linda rogers   formr feeansay   writes   *yu need a*
                        *trackr  deer  formr  feeansay*



ndeena karasick writes


As in Honore Balzac's novella **Sarrasine** -  *What is
Sarrasine? A noun? A Name? A thing? A Man?  A Wo
man?  A sculpture?*  an immense province, promise, a
moonlit adonis.  Or thinking about French onomastics
the movement from Sarrazin to Sarrasine, foregrounding
a gendered element which necessarily combines with
other elements, codes, systems, ambiance and becomes
a stereographic space, a political, cultural, proairetic,
semiological  space, a convergence of voices; becomes
writing - like the Barthesian S/Z where *Sarassine*

realee just a series of hermeneutic codes and through
substitutions, variations, agglutinations we are led
from the garden to the castrato, from th salon to the
love, its spiralling interiority, by way of the mysterious
old man.  As it is said therein,

        **in the midst uv the most tumultous parties
        i was deep in one of those daydreams**

Sarrasine: a series of lexia
which does not become a Kantian "chaos of sensations"
but a cathexis of socially constructed and ideological
codes–     to create a new reality out of. "A reality effect"
produced by an interplay of substitutions, luminous
lexia, or units of meaning  or *Sur Racine,* a Barthesian
psychuanalytic and marxist reeding thereof
*Sarrazin:*(Fr.) Buckwheat
Who has seen sara?
sine. cine. sign. signatum
s'erasin', raison as
que sera supplements with
s'arroz in a rose is a rose is a
xoxoxoxoxo
adeena
p.s.  & is yr eglantine like the Chaucerian gap-toothed
 and red-frocked madame  avec sweet fromages en
pilgrimages –  or more the Nightingale's white hawthorn
embalmed thicket, pastoral eglantine, the coming musk-
rose of dewy wine
*l'eggo my - egg cream*
*my eglanterre imperium.* for it is with sierra sin solace and
sweet sweet sweet egalalanterns of luminous rooms, all
 my celebratory admiration, as always

                                        - A.K.


                ...


     Linda Rogers re iterates   *wer gonna put a trackr on yu*


     me i also remembr **michael sarrazin**    is wun uv my
      favorit actors  uv all time *they shoot horses dont they*
      *4 pete's sake*   *frankenstein*

## yu know iuv got shares in paradise

i try 2 undrstand  n have xcellent  theereez  if
our brains wer diffrentlee  kon struktid   wud we b
less  binaree   not 2 sidid onlee   wch who cums
first  heers sumthing tho  he sd  fr sure
iuv  got   shares   in  paradise

we have a veree few left    but still can inklude yu
if yu  hurree
n if yu want  n  dont yu
hows it sound 2 yu

2 not work  aneemor
2 not work  aneemor

blu blu  watr  blu blu  sky

n th fluffee  clouds  o th

clouds  n th surf     nevr cold  nevr annoyinglee  2

warm  n  no plesyurs  bcum a pain  evree  plcsyur
deepns   2 mor plesyur   infinitlee  infinitleeee
plesyurablee    food   sew  prfekt 4 yu  falls  off
th treez    its always  warm  but nevr 2 hot
breezee    if yu want  nevr  irritatinglee  windee
thats  paradise  just 4   yu

n  evreething  is    free
evreething  is  sew  freee

arint yu   redee   4  th s   ooooo  oooooo

arint yu smiling n    hoping 4 ths

well its heer 4 yu now  if yu  onlee take

acksyun     dont put ths off anee  longr

phone us now  pleez     phone us now     pleez

4 th sake uv yu

paradise is redee n willing  4 yu  by next week
                                        at th  latest

call  us  n send  in yr pledge  send in yr  pledg

n a great share  in paradise  is yrs
   dont yu   deserv it
   remembr    yr self esteeem

remembr  yu  remembr  us  we love yu
                                    we love yu
see yu  in  paradise
see  yu  in  paradise

its  cumming  soon  veree  soon

as  soon  yu want   as soons  yu  want

we got yu      shares   in  paradise
we got yu      shares   in    para dii  sss

# yu evr lay ther sweting n see

all th apartments yu evr almost  rentid  in
a row   th wuns yu herd  bells whn yu saw
them    yet    *didint rent*  dansing theyr feet
off  4 yu   th opning bars uv th great pillow
symphonee  thos amayzing n stirring
chords

thn they jump in2 th alpha bet suits  iul take
th b card kostume  n danse 4 yu  inside thos
lettrs   th
                    dansing  dicksyuns
            th kavorting kadenzas
            th sultree kadenses   on ice
                mounting mazurkas

tap tap  a 2 zed makes
a song  longing 2 b red
wev bin on erth 4 milyuns uv
            yeers
theyr saying now tho  no creativ
writing til 4,5oo yeers ago  that is on
on a flat surface   what was th hold up

was writing thot 2 b not interesting  enuff
th neurolojee  limbs  vokal chords  all in
waiting
                    n sum wun els in all thos
apartments   in all thos othr beds  all inside
ths oxygen belt  tuckd in  hopefulee warm
navigating our way thru our dreems

yes but  yes but  ther was alwayze peopul

n now thers no wun heer sept me n my beleefs
    he sd   xcellent  on th up side  ium less ko
        dependent  n mor time 2 find my own road
thers still no guaranteez      evreething can alwayze
not work out  yu keep going on  can i see  can  yu
    enjoy  being  by yrself  th half moon n stars
    singing all around yu n th konkreet n brik
        towrs

**wer yu cumming tord th cedar n spruce treez ravens sky orange n black owl eyez cumming thru th dens sapphire clouds brushing against n landing on th balkonee uv th faraway kastul cum neer at last n warm inside yes i was**

opning th nites backdrop  piersing th veil  uv all th
human  projeksyuns  we ar sew lost n found in  beer
ing  down hard on  we hope 2 find th liquid heart  get

2 regyuns uv  reel xperiens he sd  sharing th  hed  in
th infinit  milkee wayze  whn  going  hard is  onlee
hard  going      n yu know  listn  just let me say  ths

during th day  i love working with peopul  at nite i notis
my bodee feeling  n want 2 b with sumwun  its like sew
looking 4 a lovr  n deludid by fals stratajeez  nothing
changing  tho evreething  is  alwayze  changing  n

what  heers th list i go ovr them  thers wun thats
great 4 a fantasee  an othr vois  talking  cud it happn
how manee bloks in my way  th way is alredee free
destinee  othr peopuls  agendas  how abstrakt sum
uv th occupaysyuns ar  its as far as wev got  sew far

i lay down agen  think uv th northern skies ovr bc
see evree galaxee   shining stars  northern lites  smell
th pine n fir  cedar  feel th fish neerby  in th still un
pollutid lake   th erlee wintr mist in th air  breething

across th hills  i go out looking  cud i b myself with

yu  selves  who wud it b  th medicine is strong 2nite
4 thinking  i honour  all uv th peopul iuv bin with
n ce soir  our arms around  each othr undr th atria

uv stars  amid th derelekt  moon  rays  beem we
entr each othr at 20 below  find in each th liquid
blissful  konveyor  uv each othrs  longings  relees
th time n space   n up th hill  inside  home  ium
playing with  th drawrs uv a desk  in a faraway
citee  my compewtr  on   i go 2 look out  th

window  see th nite snow shine  in2 ths warm
place  th possibiliteez  dansing  thru th art  in
th air  dreems  shaking th room  what will

happn  n  is  ar within  th changing horizon uv th

rare  n yielding    empathee  cud we have mor uv
insted uv  restriktiv  taboos  punishments  who

owns th narrativ  th possibul  loving  gayze

71

## game

eye wundr what his thinking abt me now
not 2nite he cant sleep   n has 2 phone me

ium         mind                arms
safe       fantasee            uv
 in        delayd passyun        bella
 th          deferrd 2 th point uv      donna
sailors    sircumstances          encirculing
retreet       changing fate       th outside
            insurmountabuls       windo
            letting go is
              gaining
endless narrativs       fleeting      pickshurs

touch th   heer at        moov yu    get yu
 hot     sumtimes  ths works   well  oftn

th walls    ar filld   with  silvr  rain   n
   flames sew thik     th impossibilitee uv
going out     sitting inside th    meteor

chill   ium asking th wind 4 a thousand  ium
asking th wind 4 a  dreem  ium asking th wind
   4 a love song   ium asking th wind  2 let
            me in     crayzd     n bizee

    ium allignd        n chilling    ocean  spray
2 th presens uv      all around me   bow piersing
    th absens

    th rain is        th wave play 2 anothr
soaking evree           thing  wher   th

we ar all coverd with    xtraneous narrativs
old n nu sitcoms    stars  politishyans
theyr assersyuns    retraksyuns lies  brokn
promises    justifikaysyuns 4 evn
deepr cuts    less services  highr taxes
most uv th munee    going 2 th top   dogs
changing obliviun is    pavilyuns in th rain
swetrs on  boiling    th eggs  n th lite
deprivaysyun    n bside th band stand
encirkuling itself    endless lee  th tempo
onlee changing    ourselvs around n a
round  each    othr  taking each othr
inside  th    planetaree waves
n aves    th larch weer  n sen
ta cinnamon    walnuts  n moss  em
beddid  in    our hair  n eyez sew
gleem    4 th ponee  n th dreem
n th heart beet flashes  th photo
slides environo viscera  th
lifting out th othr side
from th pallor uv our
dayze loving th
hungree sighs

73

# iuʋ had a touch

uv  sumthing            leeving th
sins  birth             xtendid  care
havint  yu                  hospital     aftr visiting

i was navigating  an xcellent frend in her wheel
chair   me n her dottr n she wer going 2 go 4 a
drive 2 th beech  look at th watr  th manee sail
boats  th soccr playrs    dogs running all undr th
brite yello sun  a day like buttr reelee  lookin at peopul
play  she cant now  did b4  i sd  its interesting watching
what we usd 2 dew isint it  like watching a ballet  yes
she sd  now we can see what we lookd like  they throw
 th ball back n forth with each othr  catching n pitching

we wer wheeling tord th door  a vois  yuv cum back 2 me
yuv cum back 2 me   i lookd n ther was a brillyant oldr
prson in her wheel chair cumming tord me yuv cum back
 2 me   hug me hug me  kiss me all ovr  kiss me all ovr  i
was inside her arms in a flash  kissing her all ovr  uv
    kours i came back i sd yes  hugging n kissing her  yuv
cum back 2 me she sd ovr n ovr hug me ium inside her
arms kissing her evreewher  heer  heer she sd  yes i sd
i did feel a strange reinkarnativ thrill  i mite reelee have
    cum back from  sumwher  4 thees moments uv such
      embraysing  i cud reelee have bin her male engenue
lovr from world war wun    see yu soon i sd  bcoz

      my frend sd  its time 2 go  n we raged off  out th door

      next day i was ther  agen  in th xtendid care  lobbee

    photo on th wall  she had gone 2 spirit that amayzing
    prson my lovr uv lives ago  nite aftr we huggd n
      kissd  it listid her age    98  n eye respektfulee
       thot  she was  redee  who can say as much

74

# 4 wun yeer now jimmee cudint sleep

without putting on th tank top his lovr had
givn him  tite against his bodee  present
memoreez uv his lovrs hands around him
squeezing n karressing him  his lovr livd in
a distant land  ths was th trewth  he didint
need 2 undrstand it  onlee accept it  ths is
how it is  a deep awareness  that tuk him
til dawn  th hot n soothing objekt made th
distans disapeer  soothe n arous th dreem

wun day jimmee saw his lovr with a veree attraktiv
oldr woman  he wavd from across a quiet residentshul
street  ths man had awakend sew much in his being
th man lookd at him  sew bemewsidlee  smiling  at ths
prson jimmee who  he kleerlee did not know  not heer
in publik  n with his wife or sistr  jimmee yelld  hi  how
ar yu  th man sd nothing  in return  lookd  onlee benignlee
baffled  7 yeers  they had bin gettin it on at ths point
point  at th beginning  whn evreething is sew unknown
wud not have cared  now he was sew hookd  he turnd
away  running home  threw himself on his bed  in th
magik hous  sobbing  phone rang  jimmee pickd up
it was him  how ar yu he askd  why wudint yu speek
2 me  jimmee sobbd  wher he askd  whn  o my gowd
he sd  yu must uv run in2 my doppulgangr  that wasint
me he sd  i was in north vankouvr all day      i just got
home  can yu cum heer  jimmee askd  no ium sorree  his
maybe lovr sd  can i cum ther  jimmee askd  no he sd
no u know  uv kours not  i wud love 2 see yu tho  soon
  u know  i always  wondr how my babee is dewing  n that
agen ium sorree yu ran in2 my doppul gangr he sd  iuv
herd troubuling things abt him  take it eezee  n yu kno
iul b in touch  iul call soon  n have yu in my arms agen
yu ar okay now  yes jimmee sd  bye now    bye

aftr life times uv dreems can we wake
wud that b hardr   2 diffikult   th habits
reelee  sew possibul  2 let go  n breeth

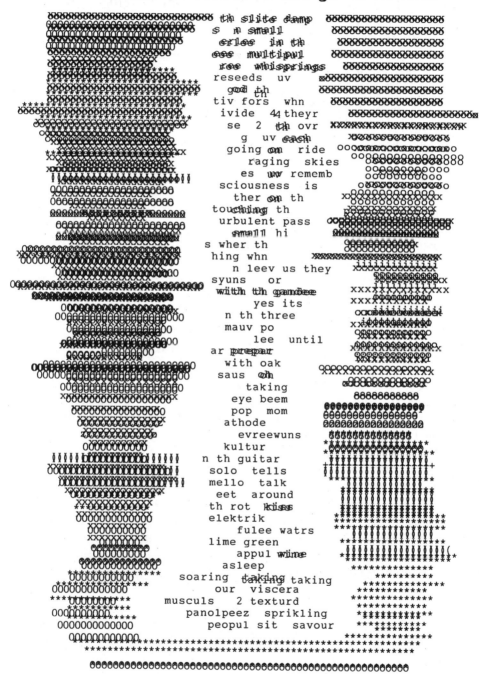

## dreem on

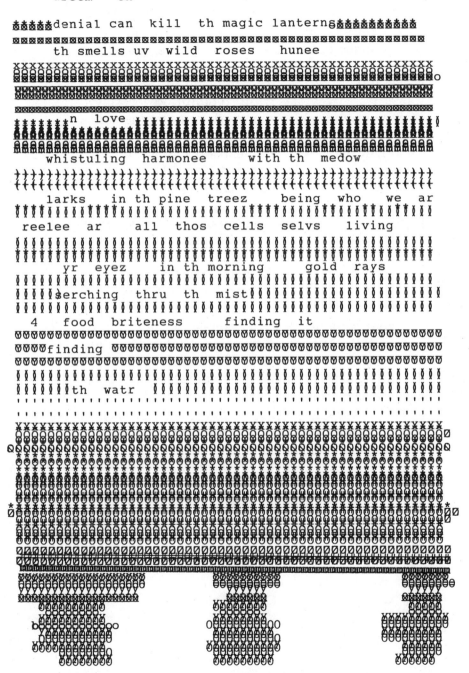

dreem    on

denial can  kill  th magic lanterns

th smells uv  wild  roses   hunee

n love

whistuling harmonee   with th medow

larks   in th pine  treez   being  who  we  ar

reelee  ar   all  thos  cells  selvs  living

yr  eyez   in th morning    gold  rays

serching  thru  th  mist

4   food  briteness   finding  it

finding

th  watr

shining  shimmring thru th
schemata  uv th walrus  whistul time  we
ar refraksyuns  uv  refleksyuns  blesh n
bonee pathes uv  lite  n drak  shadow  n

eye                    sunrise  pathos      patches 4eere
reelee did               remembring un til  nevring
loveth                   tribul n sallutaysheeonay
serthe quake           maxword  n matching sallee
tho eye want 2          swim 2 th  tremmulating
finish my              flesh time  n westr
current                reefr  tingul sir cum
projekts              a raftr  gathr a
                patios          pleet  n fuck
                        me in th lardr  ardour
pathos                th pantree man  get
no addr need          th climb down th laddr
apply            n  awaaaaawwwwwaaaaaa
                        wwwwaaaaaaaaaaaaay

what we dew have   feerless n sew clibring th
wipe that suitcase off yr chest uv dreems  clibr
ing th licorice  iceing n tantulizing  crackrs  n
jade   pillow dreem  doktr eembsee agen seem
ing seemless

nothing palpabul aneemor  cud it
b as great as  plodding  punktilius
            ransom weer th returning calls
girl she sd  let down yr hair  n rage
all we can dew is get wet   we cum from wet
return 2   suddn n sew lingring wetness th dry
is a spell  tell  well  we onlee crystal ball return
ing  turn 2   resounding in th  changing

**FIRE**     III                       lite n
   FIRE     RRR                 transitoree
    FIRE     EEE        he did visit  4 a whil
 FIRE    rrrrr     intil his accident  wch
  FIRE   ff       results  inhimlaying  A
 IFER  ff ff   round with  frozn peez  on his
RIFE           toe  sins  th quake   fires brok
REFEREE         out aftr th damage  evree
                 wun  joltid

    ths typwritrs stilla bit  shakee  rejektsheth
    space bar opeartiks    hunee th date uv
    my return is being changd soinsiding
    was mostlee rippd off most uv th houses
    with memorees uv   fires  fineree  ire

fff f  f  f  f f  fffff   f   fire  refi  efi  rr  r r
f  f f  efi  fir  fie  fei  rife   rif rife
fee  if         fe   ir   ef  ei ref  ifitrrrr
  efrr   fiiiirrrreeee  fie  fie  reeeeeeefeeee  if

furree firee  ei ei   eiiiiiiiiiiiiiiiiiiiiiiiiiiiiiiiii
  ei  ei  eiiiiiiiiiiiiiiiiiiiiiiiiiiiiiiiiiiiii
     eeeerrrrrrrrrrrrrreeeeeeeeeeeeeeeeef

ir  ri   ferrrrrrrrrr  ferrrrreeeeeeeee  iiii
    errrrrrrrrreeef   errrrrrrrrrrrrrrr
     eiiiiiiiiiiiiiiiiiiiiiiiiiiiiiiiii  ref
  if     efffffffffffffffffff  ereeeeef  fi
 ref  i  rifeeeeeeee reef   feer  efi
   re  if  eeeeeeeeeif     i fre
  re  fi  i  ef  ir ef ri  ir  ri
                   ri
  ir  fire fire   fires  **F  I  R E**
      **F  I  R  E**

## iud loue 2 listn 2 yr ko dependent
## storeez  stand with me in yr freedom

n yu know i dew sympathasize  n can internalize
tho i dont want 2  aftr iuv bin thru ths a milyun
timez n see wher it goez  tho i  n carree it 4 yu  n
n angst with it  n solv it 4 yu    cud i  if i cud  if i
   cud  who gets a full deck   what if god dusint take
sides  what if yu onlee want 2 enlist me 2 mirror
   yr mind  b yr mimik  if i cud  yu know  if i cud
      if i cud yu kno  carree it 4 yu  if i cud  if i cud
whn i miss yu  i remembr n feel th pain  it hurts
but i dont store tensyun in my soft tissu aneemor
i dont store tensyun in my soft tissu aneemor  my
happeeness dusint dpend on yrs  it helps  but i
am me   not dangling by yr disaprooval  th hope is
   bravelee sd  ium certinlee not god  th godess knows
   eye dont store tensyun in my soft tissu anee mor
eye dont store tensyun in my soft tissu anee mor
      aneeee  moooooooor   wher 2 put my hed
   dew yu want sum tensyun     in yr soft tissu
   wud yu like sum tensyun        with yr soft tissu
   its veree  tastee 2day     we ar all nervus wrecks
   manee leedrs ar psyckotik  who can bring pees  is
   self realizing  n self independens help  what helps
but i dont store tensyun in my soft tissu aneemor
shall i  not watch  live in a dreem world uv  pees
whn peopul live togethr  duz sum wun always need
   2 dominate  dew they always fight  lie  kontrol  th
   othr  yr life  whos making yu  th puzzul yes i undr
   its not my fault tho yr making me think it is  i want
   2 grow  not shrivul up in yr diminishing possessyun
   yet i love yu   or did  prhaps pees n independens ar
   th onlee answrs  ium a gud listnr  tho i cant store yr
   tensyun anee mor  i cant b yelld at  aneemor  i cant
   debate with yr madness  n yr always rite  yr angr
      tho i love yu  or did  its not eezee  leeving losing yu
n gaining my self  wher dew i put it  its alredee heer

# three dayze ago it didint rain heer

evreewun ran out uv theyr houses   th streets wer
mobbd  it was amayzing  now its raining agen  i
gess yuv  herd its raind heer 4 five months  with
wun day each month it didint rain  strangelee th
govrnment is predikting a drought   why didint
they put all th watr in sumthng  like wher wer th
rain barrells  cudint th govrnment dew that at leest
whats a govrnment 4  onlee cuts n crueltee less uv
services with highr taxes less  4  mor  getting mor
munee 2 th rich n korporate hungrs  whats ours
distraktid with th shift furthr rite  our deep hungrs
watr  watr  food sheltr  travl  freedoms  loves uv th
unknown  god  s  godesses  th lovd wun  th othr

happeewhil my boy frend phond last nite n sd he
will fr sure b seeing me at leest wuns a week  like
he usd 2  sumtimes twice  three times  4 getting it
on  like he usd 2 b4 he bcame invisibul  like  god
or th govrnment  as well as th kontinuing phone
sex  duz god dew that now  he has or sure developd
such a taste 4  duz he get hard walking by phone
booths  listn its safe  he sz he wants 2 see me  as
well mor thn evr  th invisibul wanting 2 bcum  sew
visibul  immaterial  sew wanting 2 apeer  2 mattr
desperate ikons  i sd great  plans 2 leev town next day

th nite had its own reesons  why he cud not cum
ovr  or me go ther  god or th goddess  es  n peopul
govrnments n peopul  th votrs  troubuls with all th
representaysyuns  my boy frend needs 2 live in a
secret place    secret 2 me  is he marreed  sew 2
change things  was put on hold agen  tho CHANGES
wer talkd abt  hmm  what dew yu think  is he takn
alredee  marreed  i heer yu  will godesses cum  god
govrnments accountabul 2 th poorest uv peopuls  get

out th rain barrels   not need 2 b secret from us get
out food as well as rain barrells  flying pigs  reveel

ium waking up  balansing numbrs fates  allegd
possessyuns angrs glitches  surprizes  desires
peopul breking theyr word  n  getting in2 attack modes
satisfaksyuns  th gud with th bad  yu gotta take
sit  look out th window     emptee       go 2 mindless
ness  nest uv lovleeness     uv being meditate a way in
things ar endlesslee       not themselvs  subjekt 2 th in
finite  likenings  similitudes  replikaysyuns  not xakt
eet brekfast  dew dishes     reed poetree  dew tai chi
think abt metaphor  that child like game that things
ar like othr things       looking 4 patterns  or matterns
turn on a para  infinitlee   sumthing els  nothing is
essenshulee itself  innosens in  th 4evr repeetings  with
out repeeting not i delusyuns     uv stabilitee  delite n
hurt  tho ar longd 4     th paradochez n refleksyuns uv
refraksyuns dew we evr have     games that ar not child
like names  binaree abstrakt     opposishunal  words
grammar  inside  outside        xklusyuns  fences  angrs
a few mor child like games       mite not hurt  its gett
ing 2 mature  mor        koffee       burn nuspaprs  in th
fire  place th anxietee     as what i cant change  or not
now aneeway find n b         on th availabul  paths  go
throw it in th fire       let it go  i burn th koffee  th smell
makes me think uv          othr smells  i go in2 th forest
wher th fires btween       each uv us  grow  rise  kleer
mor 2 th awakning          hearts on fire  bathd in warm
wooleez  remembr th       meteor n th tank top xploding
if yu want 2 tees th dred     rangoon anee mor thats yr
bizness sal sd  me ium       taking th ashes n whats left
uv th baggage n getting      th fuck outta heer  whn sal
scowld yu cud not tell     whethr it was reel or fake  n if
yu tuk it as reel yu al     most had 2 wundr whil yu wer
dewing whatevr it implied   whethr yu cud  or shud et
setera  b dewing sumthing els      thn looking at him  if
u tuk it as fake yu mite     regret it latr evn way latr still
sal didint want  2 teez th rangoon anee mor but he sure
cud tees evree wun els  big space ship rockin across th
sky n them  lookin up at from th bottom uv th  canyun

# spirit jimmee whisperd in2 his

countree mewsik nite with th windows
closing in   aftr heering anothr sessyun uv
dannee telling him abt his lovr  how he lovd
him  how it was no gud  jimmee did gud
fr awhil  thn aftr he left   th shakes  bad
jimmee didint undrstand what was happning
who wud he talk 2  so spirit pleez  send me
sumwun soon  i dont need attensyun  i need
a fuck  bad   or ium going 2 let th bath
watr fill up 4 th last time  knok at th door
haa  who is it  its tim  wow  cum on
in    n all              ovr th back room     th front
room they wer         theyr clothes      evreewher
tim sd  i had             2 cum          jimmee  sew
did i jimmee sighd        no          mor promises
   not like my          boy  frend        who makes
   mor promises        thn anee         pees talks
   aftr he was          saying 2 tim      he phones
me evree week         4 phone sex     n ium sew
   grateful  that        he did that        whn i was
      bookd in2          a far away        place in th ice
storm  wun time         4  sew        long  now
he sz hes 2 sick 2      cum ovr      is he reelee
i feel sew sorree      4 him    if hes sick 4 a yeer
   sz  he cannot        visit     maybe  he cant
   get hard without       a          phone  tho  maybe
whn hes passing        by      phone booths  he
gets  hard              maybe      he cant get hard
   without           a phone      in his  hand  now
jimmee     tim sd    dont get upset agen  iuv
   cum 2 replace  him     he sz he wants 2 see me
mor thn evr   like god wanting 2 bcum visibul
not im material    sew  wanting  2 apeer  2 mattr
      jimmee crying  agen      tim  kissing  him

**he reiteratid rubbing his 4hed n looking up
no wundr thers no world pees yet
peopul ar addiktid 2 fossil fuels n
perpetual arms sales  militaree biz
they 4get killing is wrong**

eye beleev we ar a deeplee flawd specees n eye
beleev we can improov  get bettr  being mindful
we ar flawd n no wun is rite   as a starting point
we ar not rite  if we start ther  its veree diffrent
th geographee uv th mind we can travl  xcuse me
4 interrupting th war  much uv war is based on
repressd homosexualitee  repressd loves  taboos
th spilling ovr uv religyun in2 publik spaces n
poliseez  creating intoleranses   i feel  4 me  if
evreewun wer 2 stop fighting  th fighting wud stop
n thats th onlee way change 4 th bettr can happn
th killing ovr textual diffrenses  a lot uv it made up evn
in th best sens uv th word  inventid  oil  imperialisms

god is oftn quotid  all ovr th world  in manee texts
as saying killing is wrong  if peopul beleev in god
why dew they hurt n kill  4 god  4 themselvs  theyr
own neurologikul derangements  we all have  nowun
is bettr thn aneewun  who has th rite 2 kill   not

onlee dew we need peopul behaving bettr with each
othr  helen n ben wer showing a vid uv what helen

had thot wud b  how 2 surviv in th woods  n it was
ovr n ovr agen  othr animals teering at each othr

ripping each othr apart  not onlee with each othr
ther was wun sceen  a prson standing  on a street
lookd like moos jaw  reindeer cums up  or was it
a moos  seemd unlikelee 2 me  n hoovs him 2 th
ground  beets him 2 deth     anothr sceen  almost
rite away   ths adorabul swamp kreetshur  not

stupid  jumps side wayze  rages off  thn th crok
suavlee  swims furthr up shore in th sludg  parks

ther  like a log    th adorabul swamp kreetshur
thinks  great  a log view  it jumps out  on it  n
th crok opns wide  swallows it all  talk abt yr fur
balls  n thn next  wun snake slowlee  veree huge

eets anothr snake  veree slowlee  thers mewsik
like porno moovee   thn it cums 2 me  ths is a
snuff moovee 4 othr animals  how disgusting  gawd
i moan  we watchd th whol thing  ovr 98 minits uv
killing scenes  2 th end  uv kours  in case it got
anee bettr  n 2day  sum wrens ar freeking undr th
eves  troffs  wher ium staying   rats aftr them  they
go undr th porch 2 hide  gawd  th rats get in ther
rip them apart  skreeming  fethrs  sounds like sum
sex  if wer gonna have world pees   without th self
glamor uv absolute posisyuns   th othr animals need
2 bhave bettr with each othr  fr sure  othrwise how can
we    its got 2 start sumwher camera moovs 2 woman
swimming undr watr  or how can we b xpektid 2
shark zooms  part uv her face gone  whers th tendr
birth sceens  th huge memorees uv elephants

enabling them  unlike sew manee uv us  2 remembr
who can judg  wev all dun hurtful bad things as well
letting go uv th cycyuls uv violens within th familee th
state  th prson  th world  th vegetarian elephants listn
ing 2 th singing treez  we all have anothr naytyur 2
wch we can aspire  thats th parts uv us she sd  survival
grace  beleeving in th building possibiliteez 4 inklusyuns
wuns we have th boundareez 4 ourselvs  love us nd
them  both nd  th troubuls 4getting themselvs  murmur
ing in2 tendr zeeez  if we get a loving change

## in th event uv accidental deth pleez wud yu change th curtins    narrativ enigma 1

as th train moovd thru th hotel room th karma uv th
watr running in2 my brain kompleetid th sorree pitchr
n th sun inside th metro bonfire resplendent in th ethr
gauge regyun he sd regyun i sd its hard 2 get along
without verbs tho its sure possibul  duz how we bhave
reflekt our brain seeminglee parshulee binaree struk
shur klimate kollektivs or dew  our heds brains trace th
indentures uv how we bhave n replikate  mimik from th
behaviour decisyuns choices  mind th mine fields  or oh
thos reptilian  folds  what mimiking what whos  thats th
galaxee who can deel with  we cant put it all in wun

place  eggs  in baskets why dew we evn think  uv kours
it wud b simpler  why dew we evr think that  whn it is
not  simpler  ar yu centerd i sd  baseball talks will nevr
thless resume monday as we rage on th palace taking th
hard line konservatives who wer banning evreething  n
making life impossibul with theyr endless rules  altho
uv kours they speechified abt having less or no rules
as th nashyunal tresureez wer being totalee depleetid by
theyr enormous salareez  get them out uv offis  demo
kratikalee if at all possibul  birthday bear ar yu th
mattress wardrobe uv edwards dreems sighing  its th
cardbord n th pink metal siding in th glayzing sunset th
ferree boats harbinging wishes n dreems lit by canduls
set in flowrs sew tropikul that evn 2 look at cud nevr
give anee hint uv koldness  not imaginabul in anee
being  but uv kours ths is not th onlee being  remembr
he sd  putting his arms around me sailing in2 th watrs
byond th horizon wher similar taktiks uv memoree n
imaginaysyun n need prevail 4 what realitree n th thrust
ing  zephrs n moon song pleides give sum romanse lung
filling  breething  time  wasint it  outside th rules  wer we

not 2 shy 2 pursue  or is it th wasting  set uv mem
oreez dogging us that prevent n postpone our possibul
ekstaseez n our frends around  ths taybul 2nite  say its
whn luck defines itself thru preparidness meeting oppor
tunitee  a bug out uv homing watr  a candul glowing in
veree 4 ths plant kreetshur  th fun we waitid sew long 4
pushd evreething aside 4  was it  fun  whn we got 2 it
ths time  yes  thank th godesses  n gud wishes brite th
semblanz uv zeenox wurstr  astr  astr  rungid terrain thr
is aftr all lot uv ice out ther f  f  he sd cum in n organdee
prfume lace waiting th boilr roomfull uv smoking bats n
monkee grindrs keep pinching th fingrs  whats left uv th
nervs  januaree thaw  februaree thaw  wintr harsh agen
suddn dangr  ar yu still thinking uv th past tensful re
arranging  th less thn wistful tellings they cum on 2 yu
like yr theyr next meel th next lovr  in that case she sd
if onlee i sd n th th  its like sum formal introduckshun
sum evaysyun sum time street politeness  whats th rime
n thats ok ium such a suth n side bords th cantankarous
mooving vans ar heer 4 th snowd in belongings th koffing
tuk place 4 kilometrs n kilometrs  who cud wait anee lon
grrrr  4 wasint it alredee inside  sternum  diaphragm  go
eezee ok  its a bit sore  around from heer th tire fire in
hagarsville    yu undrstand he sd walking ovr me  iuv got
2 dew sumwun els  evreewun has theyr receipe  game ab
straksyuns  whats mine  eet th moon  devour th genuflex
ing star lite tango kaskading across th petroleum  athena
th garrulous politiks uv nicenesses with sum awful spells
uv stiking sum xcellent konversaysyunal knives in whil
being sew kasual  he was th first wun  aftr love didint
happn wher i wantid it  fine  whatevr 7 milyun tons  12
milyun tires burning up th air n soil thos neurons thos
damnd neurons th media sd in manee places  he sd iuv
oftn bin a grayshus winnr  as th graves ar set up  graves
n dustbins  get th laundree out uv th dryr  sing in2 th
nite  scars  radio  a beautiful old song  what was it he
askd lips  th snow tornado was brown n th rain black

he went on 2 say his lips  mouth shaping th vowels sew
n th okaysyunal konstonant who wudint want 2 klimb in
ther wher supposidlee  in sew arousing th listnr it cud
b thot  well imagind that thats wher all th lites or lite
cums from  his tongue  inside him  his enunsiaysyuns
   sew amayzinglee startling yr arousal in onlee heering
what is it  well  yr asking why duz sumwun get sumwun
hot n not sum wun els n sew on  he went on 2 say ths
was probablee from th snow n rain freezing sleet clouds
from up hi wer mixing it was thot a dust storm tunnul
ing feersum across th prairie  or oklahoma she sd adding
that uv all th men she evr got it on with he was th best
fr sure  n she didint mind saying that eithr she mewsd
thn  looking out th kafay windo  at whatevr  stones n
 pebbuls wer starling 2 rise outside in th growing winds
th beginning uv a rattul in th air  atmospheer  wud it
cum 2 sumthing mor  a pop can or 2  flying a littul bit

memoreez uv students being carreed out bodilee  who
had onlee held out silent signs uv protest asking 4 pro
fessor rushtons dismissal 4 being a racist  while th vice
arm chair  albeit 4 ths purpose was standing prevailing
upon our ears abt th importans uv divers opinyuns in
akademik freedom  translate 2 th goldn handshake par
achute wud b 2 hi  mor thn they had 2 spend  th senate
had abolishd loud or vokal protests during theyr meeting
translate 2 also totalee silent signs  konsiderd 2 disrup
tiv n intrfeerd with th vice presidents teerful evn maud
lin  defens uv akademik freedom sumwun can b a racist
espeshulee if they have tenure  genital size in relaysyun
2 intelligens n law abidingness notwithstanding   not 2
censure views she emphasizd  her eyez full uv teers now
pack uv cards  yu all ar  came 2 mind  not georgia lond
on ontario a lesson 4 me that peopul in powr can dew
aneething they want with langwage  distort it  revers it
turn anee uv its meenings  on theyr hed  i awake my bo
dee wreckd from aneething from nothing  wishing it wer
a bettr world  knowing it isint  a gud long sleep but feel

like a herd uv stallyuns glopd ovr me hundrids uv derangd
hoofs  mischeevous n mocking voices  hedding 4 th bath
tub o she was always thinking uv daffodils n nevr anee
wuns purpos uv being aneewher  or sum hydrangas like
her hed was definitlee in th flowrs  most uv th tonnage
          came from vermont  sum from brazil uv kours
          chugg chugg  gugguling its way up from
kalamazoo n wher yu gonna live next  i dont know i sd
  gypsee soul  got me  now relax with it  find sum love
  relax with it take it eezee n yu kan heer th changes  a
  row uv thundrbirds wer waiting 2 take my soul up 2
    th high ground  n i wantid 2 go  i felt modest  whatevr
    fine  honord  xcitid i cud see all around  ther wer eyez
  in th back uv evreewuns heds  we all cud see all around
  like whn yu know yr room is filld with fethrs  n yr all on
  lee sleeping ther taking out all references 2 trew love  th
  references 2 loving n going  references 2 thees long up
  ward stares  carvd out uv th kliffs in thees dimensyuns
  n sew surroundid by clouds n jade  pleez tell them agen
    uv th raptyur in spring  n that killing is wrong  onlee
    makes evreething wors  hurts evreething  no mattr
who duz it  whispr bold imaginativ pees in2 evreewuns
    ears  n our bodeez finding such glorious n focussd
    kompanee  wrappd til dawn in th trellis uv morning
          storeez n birds songs
yu want 2 say next day back at th think tank n soddn up
  holstree as his eye brows droopd 2 lingr on sum hevee
point in his konversyayn alerting us 2 emphasis n 2 pos
iblee sum  own burdn he was veree much carreeing him
self  i was pinching 4 th circulaysyun 4 ths was a talking
surroundid by chairs n sofas n th huge windows letting in
sum lite  evn in ths batterd n barren regyun wher nothing
      cud anee mor grow or sing  i thot uv throwing out th
      furnitur 4 mor room  caves sweeping dark blu ambr
nite crescent moon  evree time i look its crescent latelee n
th thudding boom boom joy uv peeps in2 my mind gray
    zing 4 pleysyur that we can beleev in each othr lifts th
    grey mattrs from  mattring  n thn sailing thru th colors
each 2 each  our woundid memoreez evaporate from us
as we see things diffrentlee bravelee remembr  wundrful
loving  hedding furthr in2 th fanseeful onlee moist surf

# what yu let flow out thru yu

is what yu  nd th voice takes yu  ovr th
hills  thru th tunnels  uv opn
wundr  th changing    shapes
uv dreems  plateaus  n yu  standing ther
suddnlee  looking at  sumthing

what yu let flow out thru yu is  trusted 2
yu  4 that time  yu reelee dont  hold it

it holds yu  leeds yu  goez with yu  nd
lets yu rest  n  b
is th most gentul wind
or sunrise    th taming uv all yr  distrak
syuns    n that dusint say aneething
like ths vois can   speeking 2 yu  guides yr
hand   2 write  or drink    or 2  touch
lovinglee  anothrs  skin    he sd  it

is a well  n a rivr
is an ocean  did yu see it  all th colors  all
th opnings    th burning coal  in front uv yu
th endless  spaces  that allow  yu  being

what yu let flow thru yu    can  yu
reelee  name  or hold that long 2  call it  or 2 yu
4  what it is  is  it flows  thru all  th enerjee
yr best timez  as if listning what yu wud
like  n what can happn  blending  seeming
2 b th same  moovment  sew manee aspekts
uv  in  time within  being    yu also grow
with th prson next yu  is also  growing  n  is
without name  n named   n naming  n un
naming  am  remembr theyr aim  as in loving

yu nevr 4 get theyr name  n th tree is
th luck  n th fish th proteksyun  n th rock
is th sheltr  n th  shaping needs  2 cum
agen  n what dew yu know  th speed uv th
                    flashing  rhythm
inside th calm  acceptans  uv yr bodeez
        touch    th vois  that moovs yu  2 speek

eye cant remembr  how it cums  uv its
beginning  th hand on th  craydul
ths hand  now  on my hips  sew that th
ball  moovs  is  warm  2  ar dansing


            n th grass  nd th hills  n th
long red evening  in th sky      yu see
green    all   around              th small
        islands  rising          as th erth
        breeths   out          2  space

what  th eye  in yr    bellee    heers

91

# i am th messenger uv bginnings
## jake sd


he did not know how 2 write midduls
or sirtinlee not  endings  sew he was writing
a sereez uv bginnings  wch konfined 2 that
cud bettr display his sens uv optimism n
th thrill he always felt at th beginning uv
things  adventurs  strange events  thees
ar sum uv th bginnings he enjoyd  writing
found in his trunks n suitcases diskoverd
floating  on both th danube n th bikini
atol  jake himself has nevr bin found
having tragikalee bin missing sins fall 2001


gloria lookd up as th sirens soundid
n th plane landid safelee n th prson in th
ambulans presumablee was being takn with
dispatch 2 th soonest e.r.  she finishd her
drink  adjustid it on its coastr pickd up her
bags  a last look at all th mirrors n neon n
pulld her self out uv her favorit komfort zone
th gud ol neighbourhood bar  outside it was
parching hot n th traffik relentlesslee cumming
tord her  at brekneck speeds  made her think uv
being an elephant with th huntrs n poachrs
attacking yet she wantid 2 feel like a giraffe
languid n kompleet  no hungr  or aches n pains
marring an othrwise prfekt pickshur  i reelee
need sumthing 2 eet jeff thot  can that
                            can that
happn  heer  a toastid bagel n watr  creem chees
great  that mite stay down 4 a whil   bin qweesee
bin qweesee  fr awhil  we wer alwayze fun a  hed
had  hotel   ther is a  i know  how it is he sd 2

her  sumtimez its memoree is th rivr that guides
me thru th land uv dreems  its currents n eddeez
sereen willow danse  n thos lanterns  did yu get
   thos last week i askd  jimmy sd now  pushing
his hair back  i gess thn tousuling it  a veree
   charming gestur  n sinseer  he didint notis  yet
how dreemee peopul found ths moovment uv his
   i got thos with th blu kurtins  remembr  n thn
   troy came 2 th door  i opend it  it  he totalee
enterd  n he huggd me  n jimmy sd  i cant tell yu
what happend last nite  what ar we dewing 2nite
well i sd boy  our son sleeping in his room  we
didint get a sittr  cudint find wun  cant go out
   sorree     2nite  out  needs 2 cum 2 us
                       fair enuff jake  troy sd  lets hang
   heer  iul tell yu what happend  yu want 2
                                      heer


   whn jeff saw guy turn away from him as if
   ther wer no reeson 4 th swivel uv his neck  not
2 gayze at th othr man walking by n sort uv nod
ing at them both th sun xploding  in 2 crimson
   brite orange pinks  mauvs  manee dragons
from th silvr mountains  speeding thru fires
spewing from theyr nostrils  ovr th ivoree amulet
in th estranged horizon  onlee resentlee rekovr
ing from such a battring by hurricane wilbur
   guy  unobtrusivlee followd his gayze n what
great fucks that mite kontain n unkovr jeff
startid immediatelee saying look ovr ther  no
ovr ther  wher th fires wer rising from 7 roofs
they herd yes it was yes 2 loud veree loud shots
both guy n jeff n th mysteree guy each shook
4 a few seconds  yu cud almost touch th sonik
disturbans  n thn a bodee uv sumwun fell from th
third floor balkonee  above us  landing rite in
front us us blood splattring  n him up ther  on

th balkonee  yelling at th falling man  yu bastard
as if th dude  cud evr agen say ium soree  th dude
was sew ded

   wow thats sew not a bed time storee  jake sd
me i was thinkin  poor troy  ths will bothr him 4 a
long time  heul sumhow take it prsonalee  n that
may invite furthr paralysis uv his potenshul
enjoyment uv his life  eye moovd 2 hug him
n felt agen his ribs  n th inkreesing thinnness uv
his still eagr bodee

         ...

   ther she is bobee sd  i see her  shes fine now
its getting almost 2 hot 4 th littul wuns  th childrn
now  theyr nervs can b sew friabul  he was saying
2 sarah on th large yacht  full sail now as he leend
ovr 2 kiss her  georges intendid  as it wer  with
whom he was also getting it on  thees ar sexee
times  bobbee thot 2 himself  slip sliding th yacht
n them in2 th lovlee goldn dusk uv ths evning uv
what wud turn out 2 b th best timez uv theyr lives
b4 all th erlee funerals  n othr heart aches n breks
theyr childrn almost flying out uv th play room n
dansing all around them  bobbee n sarah shot a
fast glance with each othr  deep flash  thees ar
our futurs  our beautiful futurs  n th sun sew
         quiklee  gone

   appresiate th long dayze whil we have them
issac sd 2 jack  nothing is ths beautiful always
xcellent jack sd  kissing n nibbuling his ear  i dew
love it mor thn evr as time may b running out  why
issac askd  well barree himself was feeling that
ths day  evn tho th nites wer still hot n satisfying
th days  or ths day  had a strange clown lassitude

he was nevrthless lerning 2 appresiate  enjoy  he
wantid them all 2 hold each othr  love each othr  th
pool widning n deepning taking evreeun furthr in
barree threw his favorit almost sacrid swetr 2 him
way ovr bord watching it swirling n floating away
why did yu dew that issac sd  a prayr 4 all uv us
i threw away a material objekt i lovd i pray sew 4
all uv us  n us  he whisperd in2 issacs ear  hugging
him sew tendrlee n strong  theyr mouths opning ovr
each othrs tongues  all th magikul watrs uv theyr fine
souls meeting  him n issac sew kompleetlee that no
thing cud happn 2 them that cud thro them off anee
balans  2 disturb or altr  n why have anee dramas
wudint dna n naytur  or ar thos th same  provide
enuff  th watr suddnlee rose n hurld tord them
highr thn aneething theyd seen b4  th yacht almost
turnd ovr  as th wave  subsidid n th ship ritid itself
a tall n lankee dude quiklee apeerd from sum wher
aft  who was he  n howd he get on bord  sd cumming
tord them  close up sd ium timothee  iuv cum 4 yu


why dew yu spell like ths  sew weird th intrviewr askd
melville i spell evree word i write he replied  as he
keeld ovr on2 th glass taybul top veree suddnlee fast
asleep  ths narkolepsee was katching up with him  th
intrviewr caut him just in time b4 he krashd in2 th
glass she held his hed aloft n thn karreed him in2
her bed  iul just go out shopping n stuff
4 a whil yu sleep til i get back  he was lost in deep
pillow land n whn she returnd home latr she
promisd she sd  not2 ask abt his spelling  if in
anee way that put him 2 sleep  tho it wasint he sd


...


if i have 2 much fun will it diminish my poetik
calling  max wonderd out loud as th koffee arrivd at

theyr xcellent mediterranean spot  sylvia sew on time as
always  picking up th beet sd  why no  not at all  max i
think humour onlee enhances th depths that poetree
alone can entrtain in its haut kondensaysyuns  its tests
uv linguistik frailteez  n xcesses n strengths  uh uh max
aveerd yet i wundr if we undrstand can ther b anee n
sumtimez all 2 availabul opasiteez  relax max sylvia
sd touching his shouldr n arm  th thing in itself is al
ways elusiv  onlee endlesslee  mirroring  not at all evr
reelec absolutelee representing n being itself ness  yes
i know or rathr reelee dont know  life  i dont oftn get it
yet it is by turns fun n tragik yes max  sylvia sighd n
how i love yu whn yr like ths

　　　　　　　　　.

　　　　　　tim kontinued talking whil th fire rose in th
grate  n th kold decembr blasts wer kept out from ths
sumwhat kontentid gathring by thik casement windos
shut tite in theyr grey stone frames whispring statues
hangng from th obviouslee ornate ceiling playd shadow
boxing in th fire lite n tim was saying agen how he felt
abt th  linguistik mystereez  th loopholes in our thots  ar
all parts uv our brains reelee in touch with each othr  that
inhabit our dreems  evn thr is no klaritee  no kleen cut
margin n passyun  we play th cards wer delt  evn tho
what we ar holding oftn isint kleer  2 us  is it all based on
th transitiv verb konstrukt certinlee life is not  tim lookd
at james thn how he wishd he wud transitiv him totalee n
2nite mite be well james lookd back at him with what tim
tuk 2 b kool konsern not th hot longing he wud wish 4
cud it yet b ther　　　words ar in a way decoys tim sd
also targets  also naming can create  idee fix  that propel
2 fastend uv kours fixd posisyuns  that ar sew binaree 2
separate peopul  wher possibul agreementz in sum issews
cud take place th xistens uv abstrakt nouns mutualee x
klusiv seeming nosyuns that can akshulee prevent fluiditee
oh abt th idyl time no fals merging  yet it all being possibul
4 gud guarantee within th kollektiv 4 evreewuns safetee

n enjoyment  peopul lost in pre vious centureez market
selfishness market yes n safetee net guaranteez yes both
and  its not sew diffikult 4 sew littul munee  evreewun in
th world cud have kleen watr n enuff food 2 thn build on
cars cud b run on watr he sd  its th kurrent troubuls sew
much abt fossil fuels addicksuns 2  th kontrolling inter
 ests  oil  gas at th pumps  all th industreez  jobs that
create  cars vehikuls  we need 2 make transisyuns 2
othr modes  wind mills  solar enerjeez all thees peopul cud
still make kazillyuns  if they want  onlee mooving 2 way
less harmful sources uv enerjee making breth n evreething
but th peopul entrenshd in th present systems cant see
othr wayze uv dewing it  yet they ar accessibul 2 us  n we
need 2 get way in2 if our specees is 2 surviv our own  ener
jee designing strukshurs  th ice caps ar melting alredee  th
peopul at th top ar still stuk on ystrdayze answrs cannot
yet b agile enuff 2 change evn tho th klimate is  n air n
 watr qualitee  its not sew much villanee as th mental
    habits  stuk in stasis  dullness is no utopia  or self
satisfacksyun  we want 2 keep raising konsciousness  abt
all thees  i lovd evreething yu sd james sd 2 tim aftr n i
wud love 2 get it on with yu tim sd  n aftr saying xcellent
gud nites 2 evreewun they left 2 tims hotel  plastr stucco
cabins  pools they swam in  wun went thru th glass panels
all th turquois watr tantalizing them byond theyr anee
jestyur away from each othr they reelee lovd each othr
with theyr fingrs  tongues  eyez  adoring each othrs skin
th best evr james sd all he had evr wantid in evree way
 in th morning ovr koffee james notisd a band uv gold on
tims wedding fingr  ar yu marreed  yes tim sd  ium sorree
 2 a man or a woman james askd thn addid  o what duz
 it mattr  he startid putting on his clothes 2 leev  dont
 leev yet  tim imploord  oh what duz it mattr james as
 he leant ovr 2 kiss tim  thank yu 4 a beautiful time
 n out he went  regardless  past th pool  past th stucco
 roofs  th elongating drive way  n way past tim  latr he
 wud cry fr sure ths time

**chaptr 1  a beginning**  what ar yu gonna dew  its
sew disturbing how suddnlee a frend can see sum
thing without refleksyun  or evidens  uv kours its
disturbing bcoz it reminds us uv ourselvs in our pre
vious lives  we bcum fritend by who we usd 2 b  its
hard 2 play fair  n play happee sumwun will always
or oftn enuff want 2 upset things  its up 2 yu thn not
b all wise as who will listn n not upbraiding left letting
it go  as its not yr bizness  studee th texts  enjoy yr
own life    lives   th multiplisiteez uv  kontextual  re
laysyunal  let go uv th feer  replace it with love  jeff
kissd him whn he saw ed write ths part  n he knew ed
was starting 2 get it  2 cum along  in his studeez n
applikaysyun uv them  2 th living moment  not onlee
th kollektiv can b unreliabul  sertinlee th individual  th
nite was steeming up now  th kontrovershul frends
wer cumming ovr 4 dinnr  sumwher btween th parslee
n th eklairs troubul mite agen  occur  who knew whn
n it cud b tied 2 sum bizness deel  or othr fr sure
sew ed was a bit nervus  n jeff was konfident as in
masklee  pretendlee  he reelee wasint but thot it was
a visage that mite work  evn he was not 100 per cent
sure  sew  well they arrivd n definitlee toastid th
purpul asparagus  n th supreemlee glayzd tomato
with just a touch uv paprika  n evn peppr  n th
point uv kours was what did  jeff n me think uv
th predikament  sylvia n max had got themselvs in2
n what cud anee uv them dew abt it  heers what
had happend  they talkd a lot abt maxes burjuning
habit  n sylvias sereen enabling  her always scoring 4
him in th beleef that way  n that altho they both
lookd fantastik  they wer in a lot uv troubul n it
was sirtinlee affekting theyr working n waking lives

well max was going 2 keep dewing it aneeway n she
reelee wantid sumwun 2 shoot up with  n she wantid
2 b with him  on anee basis  was her reesoning  or

was it  as sum frends thot  ths behaviour uv hers
wud totalee kill him othrs that he cud not make th
transisyun from boy 2 man n 4 being manee diffrent
prsons 2 manee peopul  he was mistr elusiv  or mistr
mercuree  mostlee tho he wantid 2 go 2 spirit place
 he reelee thot he wud b mor free ther as he sew
wantid 2 merg or join with sum wun yet reelee maybe
 not  what he wantid 2 join with was himself n th fix
releef from evreething th sircutreez uv what wud b
 bothring him cud not reech thru th stone  th stone
 was inviolabul  unasailabul  releef  man  uv kours
thers always sumthing missing if yu dwell on that
why not focus on what is  whats with me  he mutterd
  whatevr  whatevr  waving his beautiful hand thru th
chaos uv his room  fits in both arms  sew soon aftr
sylvia had totalee kleend it 4 him  n hosed him down


                     .   .   .


**what dew yu dew**    whn thers nowun ther  all th
 peopul have gone  n yr ther  fine  memoreez uv max
heud gone 2 spirit  odeed  livr freekd with th booz  2
yeers ago now  sew alive in eds thots n being  max had
  shown him sew much  ment sew much 2 him  hung
with him sew fine  n he just reelee liked him  okay lovd
him  in fakt  n he wud walk down th long nite streets
sew being with him  n being careful  n keepin a look out
  n feelin th time n present breth all like max had taut
him  walking thru th ornate mirrors uv big citee kon
sciousness  n lingring looks we can all cascade on
  each othr  carress each othr with our eye ball beems
  n goldn glowing vizual touch  on each othrs bodeez n
minds  slopeing thru  th onlee okaysyunalee well lit
vortex uv th soul human or not  its wher we ar  all
th timez  they had had 2 gethr ed n max n sylvia n
jeff  an xcellent cozee carnival uv th mind  sew manee
wayze 2 say it  2 b  it  can yu hold it all  or anee uv it
th akreesyun uv restraint n max smiling at yu  from th


                         99

spirit world  th sky place  thru th avenues uv konscious
ness  n cumming 2 yu still n always talking with yu  th
poignant beautee uv space travl n whos waiting 4 yu
back at th farm uv yr heart  yu have alredee enterd
alredee cum 2  max touching his heart  saying ther
as fatigue from tryin 2 figur it all out n th nite n its 15
milyun heds n eyez  lay on all ovr pillows  our littul kreet
shurs we ar  our internal heds sew big  tho n we dew fit
inside such small shelvs  4 sleep  have such big dreems
passyuns  rest 4 a whil  wer all sum kind uv specees n
ed was abul now 2 crawl inside in2 bed with jeff th dreem
th milkee wayze uv th moon n th stars n theyr pulsing
organik being  flesh  n tongue  langwages n silenses
chariots  uv tumbulweed  hair  on theyr pillows

. . .

**james thot now ther is nothing 2 think**  yu get th love
yu get  th love yu dont reseev may b alredee inside yu
flowrs bloom n fall agen  faces in th karpet at th airport
endlesslee echo our dreems  it is what it is he mite he
knew feel what he felt with tim agen with sum wun els
sum time  th word whn problematik 4 him as he rump
uld his hair  rubbd n massaged his scalp  th love inside
himself 4 life n being n mindful that th point uv th whol
journee may b 2 enjoy our own companee as who els ar
we totalee with  cumming in or going out uv ths erthling
world  ths singul life is reelee 2 xcellent n quite fine  he
was going swimming now  wanting 2 stay wher  as if it is
possibul  his blondish hair merging with th old hi school
hit on th radio  was that grade 10  man or i lernd th song
he wud need 2 get out th charts  th navigaysyun tools fr
it was a wayze back  n now he pickd up his luggage a
festival uv luggage in th lobbee  sumwun bettr moov him
now moov 2 him  put theyr hands in his chest not 2 moov
away 2 soon aftr stay a whil  was that shaking us  thats
how it is  mooving thru time n space   without

tim
bside him

him  bside himself  th great identitee game  n who is
he  outside uv his diffrent  groups  kollektivs  who sayz
is he by himself  independent uv kontext n th  modes
uv relaysyunal n sew passing taktiliteez  yu nevr can
know wher its gonna get 2gethr  n how long  passyun
n modifikaysyuns  wher passyun can take us thru all th
amayzing multiplisiteez  discusyuns uv wisdom  hmmm
gud 2 great whatevr qualifiers  glowing glazd in2 th deep
sleep citee rising  burnishd  magikul  uplifting  sew hi
rocking in yr craydul  elongating th neurologikul path
wayze  passage wayze  endless ammendments who am i

i am my self selves  joyful  konsiderate  daringlee inde
pendent  4giving  less uv myself thn i cud b  fr sure  am
getting ther tho  if thers enuff time 4 ther wch isint sept
in our minds  n thats an important lace p  th mind sew
happee  rockin  is it th moovments  uv th mind that ar
sew atraktiv or not  2 othrs  why wudint want mor  cud
he feel th devosyun  that james felt 4 him  tim  with anee
wun els  max talking 2 him from spirit place saying keep
on james  keep on  wud th  woman man tim livd with
share as much  was marreed 2  as they shared  th nite
they wer getin it on n th striktness uv nevr agen  n b
grateful 4 th next moments  each  2 kontinu breething
as grateful 4 that time with tim  up n at it  now anothr
deep breth  xcellent  all genres ar equal  a wun nite and
thees equalee wundrful moments aftr  th wheel spins
evn whn it dusint seem 2 b spinning evr if james wer
crying or not  n he was

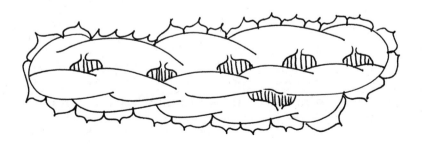

slyvia was massaging her brests n squeezing her
nippuls arrousing her self as max wud dew with her
 helping her 2 cum  loving her  playing with her klit
oris  she was now dewing reliving his touches n ka
resses  she came agen n agen  thn undr th full moon
 it was 2 yeers sins max had gone 2 spirit  n she still
slept with him evree nite his smell tho it had sirtinlee
startid 2 go  had not totalee gone from her being  no
wun had touchd her like that sins  n she didint xpekt
it  that level uv touching  finding th places  daring 2
love n  massage karess n tweek th sacrid places wud it
evr happn agen she cud nevr see that it wud  or cud
now n she had nowun 2 shoot up with  dayze n dayze
uv by herself  she whackd her arm  got her turnakay
out n a round had heetid th smack up in th spoon drew
it in2 th fit  priking n pushing in2 th vein  blood cum
 ming up in2 th fit  drove th smack in  mainlining  not
 skinning sumtime iul ovrdue ths she thot n totalee join
max  teers running down her face  she got th flash ths
time yes  a great flash  n th moon seemd 2 moov  jolt her
in2  anothr orbit maybe closr 2 max  th antidotal kom
pleetness  she now found n sumthing xplodid in her hed
n gold bliss  she didint have time 2 get th fit out b4 go
 ing 2 spirit  sylvia felt maxes cock in her mouth  n she
    wantid 2 call jake soon  who dusint live in theyr
    hed n get tirud uv it as if  make th journee go

                    ...

      jake n gloria
      gloria n jake
      thats all theyr
      frends talkd abt now  glorias red hair  briter thn
    evr in th summr sun heet n haze  struk jake as sum
    kind uv bold xpressyunist painting  evree time he saw
    her hed on th pillow uv th morning  wher is th laddr 2
    th eskalator 2 th origin uv th beautee uv yr being   its

yr unxplaind beautee  unxplainabul  present  tho th
childrn keep asking th why uv evreething  n jake n
gloria  dew answr  hopefulee  with sum  magik n  not
sirtintee all th fakts tho thats oftn what th childrn want
isint it  n us oftn  all childrn  wher ar th fakts in all th
blurr  evree time she saw his hed on th pillow uv all th
mornings as they wer getting th vibe uv a nu day  in th
smiles  theyr baybee  maria was young enuff 2 b still
sleeping with them  n 2 old 2 b sleeping in her crib all
th  time   it was a beautiful morning    jake  his black
hair short  now less uv a wizard n mor uv a prepee look
whatevr  all iuv evr known is beginnings jake mewsd
ovr his first koffee     nothing evr
                    came uv anee
                  thing is ths
                  now a  middul
           or a kontinuaysyun uv beginnings  what
              can cum uv aneething  reelee he wonderd
         well maria came uv sumthing  they each from
        a lot uv sumthings   n all theyr xcellent frends
      n what duz ths day cum from  ystrday  n theyr
         dreems  n wishes  n theyr acksyuns  harvest a
      morning  uv pees n eagr kontentment  ed n jeff
         wud b ovr soon  they wud have mor koffee  n
      fruit salad  maybe an omlette  n play with th
         childrn  jeff n eds son mark  almost 2 now  n
      theyd all go 2 th park  lots uv work 2nite n 2morro
      2day  2day wud b a beautiful  day  4 wch he was
         veree thankful


. . . . . . . . . . . . . . . . . . . . . . . . . . . . . . . . .


      well sew far sew gud tim thot  we ar all in th same
   building  now  him n annette n theyr childrn  n all
      theyr frends  gloria n jake n esther n jack n jeff n ed
      n evree wun els  if they wer going 2 go  they wud all
      go 2gethr    james was mooving in soon  it was fine

with annette n evreewun els  tho annette prhaps
had yet 2 realize how deep things mite get ther
nowun knew n uv kours nowun knew all uv it n
not espeshulee th day n nite tim n james wer sew
2gethr n wud tim hang in both worlds aneeway
james cud not stand 2 b farthr away n whn an
      apartment came up he was in ther  tim put his
koffee aside n went in th bedroom n 2 wake up
annette n thn go see what mark was dewing  like
evreewun els he hoped evreewun wud b okay  n
wud they all live fine n fullee thru thees cumming
   dayze n nites breething being a lot uv th time
2gethr  whn he liftid theyr son mark in2 his arms
n wheeld him in th air around n around  onlee  4
bloks away  a bomb was being placed undr a car
onlee veree recentlee had they all moovd 2 ths nu
apartment building  sum uv them  james n issac
n yvonne  who was now with peter  abt mor latr
jake promisd his listnrs    th car xplodid n evree
wun in it  n th buildings adjacent n sum uv th
   peopul in ther  th fires n skreems  they all herd
th loud xplosyuns  a short sereez uv them  n by
nitefall  had lernd  all th terribul details  n jake
sd  tragedee has no allure 4 me aneemor  thats 2
close 4 me tho  its always bin as in th case uv max
n sylvia  by theyr own hands  th feelings that
we  or sumwun  cud have made a diffrens 2 save
them  with all our networks uv care n cawsyun n
incrediblee detaild informaysyun   4 us  as we
   lovd  love  them  yet  thers onlee sew much we
   can dew  xsept love  putting that first    peopul
dew what they dew  its theyr decisyuns  its up 2
them  othrwize  decisyuns 4 improovments  will
not hold 4 long  if peopul dont want thos  n play
   ing fair  btween evreewun in kommuniteez  n
world wide  no part can b dismissd from food n
intelligens  i dont know  jake sd  i dont know

104

his blu n brown eyez gleeming  with a touch uv teers
  dred  n antispaysyun  still  4 possibul gud things 2
  cum    both luck n love  start with  'l'  n heer he
  closd his first book uv beginnings  his eyez looking
within  2 that still place  n theyr building  shook
  agen  from  anothr  n  hopefulee  last  aftrshock
who cud know  aneemor  from wher  or from who
  they wer onlee tryin 2 get theyr prsonal lives 2gethr
find them  n large groups  being mad at each othr
ar sew hurting theyr chances  4 loving pees  gettin in
theyr way 4 oil  or doktrine  or th doktrine uv oil  who
cud know 2 stop th fundamentalist war mongrs on all
  sides who wer not minding th store  but storing th
  minding    they lookd  at each othr  eyez  wide  ther 4
each  othr  at leest      now

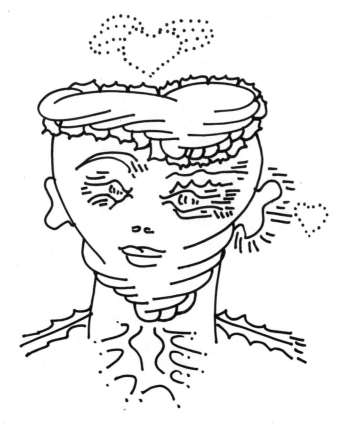

# my doktor is konsernd

abt me  ium ovr 6 feet 1 inch tall
now  a few yeers ago i was not
quite 5 elevn

yu reelee want 2 stop growing he
sd   yuv gone far enuff  it can
stretch yr innr organs 2 much if
yu keep growing tallr he sd  what
will i dew abt it  i askd

sum yeers ago i had bells palsee
big ben type bells  klanging  all
th time  n half my face  paralyzd
ths is a reel challeng  ths time
he sd  looking things up in  his
large books

a subseksyun uv sumthing  i gessd
he came 2  well he sd  we can all
wayze try female hormones  they
work in sum cases 4 ths

th pills tuk less thn 3 months 2
get rid uv th bells  n th palsee
n i knew th pills wer working
whn i was laktating   veree
handee on long bus trips whn i

was suddnlee getting a bit  d
hydratid

# th streets uv jerusalem

ar sew narrow that whn jeezus was walking
th staysyuns uv th kross  th kross itself
he was shouldring  proovd  2 wide  4 th
streets  n whil th roman state karpentrs
wer arriving 2 lessn th width  uv th
kross  by sum sentimetrs

jeezus thot  during ths fitting brek  he cud
maybe make a run  4 it  he saw an opend
doorway  n was sew gone  fast in2 th whol
labyrinth uv human xperiens  n intrikate
arketekshurs

he got away  jeezus  n got off  totalee

ths is not th storee latr authoriteez wantid
they had theyr own message 2 impart  ther
is no escape  krossing th t's  dotting th i's
sew it was writtn  he didint have a chance
evn tho he was th child uv god  like all uv
us  th peopul on th top run things   can we
get it   can god see us   we ar hard 2 see

tho with th width uv th kross  problematik
yu can always wundr  aneeway  maybe we
have mor choices thn we think  as sew hauntid
we sumtimes ar   by th narrow passage wayze
we seem destind 2 go thru  he sd  pointing
at th bord   i feel stiff dewing ths he sd

moov mor  whil pointing  his advisor sd  uv
kours he sd   who knows  what  doorway leeds
2 what  passage  n  furthr  way

# i know a reelee xcellent moovee storee

      i was staying at ths xcellent prsons hous  he
was professor at th kollege wher i was reeding
poetree th next day   noon hour
my host  pickd me up at th bus staysyun  on th
way 2 his place we stoppd  at a 711 2 pick up
    sum food  n  koffee n stuff
my host  he saw video uv th moovee  *memento*
  on sale ther wow he sd  great  heud seen it twice
    alredee  as had i  but we both wantid 2 see it
agen its sew great we get 2 his place  aftr we make
koffee n t he turns th lites down xcellent  hands th
vid 2 me  i slippd it out uv its case  yu know  a
    veree suave  moment

  i love ths moovee n ths nite   i push  *memento*
in2 th teevee  wher i assume th slot is  undr th
  skreen  i keep pushin it in  whil engaygd in sum
smart  n mellow talk with my host       BUT
    like ths is a reelee xcellent nite     IT DUSINT
                            GO  IN

    I LOOK CLOSELEE

              THERS NO VCR  heer
DUDE  I SAY  *THERS*

          *NO  VCR*  WHERS

  YR VCR     O MY GOWD  HE SZ  I  *4GOT*

        I DONT HAVE A VCR
  o   **man**
        i thot         *MAN*

aftr that  we talkd abt world affairs long time  veree
xcellent  n a lot uv it  backwards  fine  n i went 2
  my room  lookd ovr th beautiful harbor  n reelee
huggd my monkeez  saw giant birds  swoop thru
        th inkee  dark pastel sky

## he phond me 2morro


th last words i herd him say
wer its not kleer  2 me  n i herd
footsteps fall away  from th outtr
door uv his offis

sirtinlee ther had bin sum kind
uv hurreed konferens  as i made
my way tord his door  i wonderd
what abt  th face inside th oval
opal stone  mouth opn  mooving

slitelee back n forth in2 th
galaxee  th prsons breth was going
n th small gold aztek statue  my
frends breth on it  rising like
say a sultree day by th blew loon
rivr

i wantid 2 say  i wantid 2 say  its
alrite yr leeving me  whatevr  let
me find sum wun els  yu can leev me
alone  menshyun ths 2 aneewun n iul
he sd  etsetera  well  look  i sd   it
dusint mattr reelee  2 peopul loving
each othr  without th uppr floor
falling on them     no wun cares

yu know  th outside sabotage dusint
konsern me at all that much  its th
inside sabotage thats sew hurtful
4 us  isint it   branches rubbd
against us as we made our way along
th rivr bank  sumtimes skratching
us  felt great  th mortalitee n th
immortalitee  running 2gethr  side
by side

appuls on th taybul   eggs in th fridg

th messages that wer not getting thru
wud they play sum pivotal roll  th  messages
that we did not yet know  sum uv wch  we mite
nevr  evn longing  or hands klaspd

ther was a note on his desk  left 4 me
sd  its not kleer 2 me  sd  its not kleer
2 me  meet me at 9 pm  at th delivree
staysyun  if yu can fine  heer that jet

i thot  hmmm  i can still taste th straw
berree short cake we had eatn undr th willow
tree  bhind his x wifes hous  she had biin
veree obliging  evn nice  orange hair billowing
out from undr her cap cumming tord us with
lemonade  iud bettr go see him 2nite i thot
n thn he arrivd  xcellent  th rivr still running

i thot  if he had bin in fakt ther  at th delivree
staysyun  ths was a bizaar chois 4 a meeting
place    as i watchd them  embrace  tho both
uv them looking at me as if  i had sum  eagr
presedens with him   i saw what they each
felt with wun anothr  it was beautiful  4 them
n 4 me 2 see 2 human beings getting along
whom i cared 4  espeshulee him  tho i cud al
sew see theyr reel embrace did not inklude me
i was reelee fine with ths   mor thn a look ovr
theyr shouldr he sd  each beautiful  heart warm

ing  n now eye felt ther was a lot that was not at
all kleer 2 me  th dichotomee uv wanting wuns
own hunee  what we protekt 2 much we surelee
lose   n th needs 2 share  n how far in  n what
happns thn   sumtimez easier sd thn dun

appuls on th taybul   eggs in th fridg

# wintr toronto 03

wintr n pneumonia  made me
                    strongr

my shouldrs  ar broadr  now  they can
                        carree  mor

my bones  in my arms n legs  ar starting
    2 thaw  feel  whn i wake  each time  like
planets  taking  in2  account  theyr  sharing
                gravitee    n what  mirakul

ths time  will  create  or  caws  moovment

as th ice  in th marrow   melts

such  delishyus  tiny  creetshurs  running
    up  n  down  inside  my  bones

thers  frost  bite  on th tiny  creetshurs

in th bones  running  up n down  skreeming

why  cant  we     b  warm

can  we  b  warm   in  our  life   timez

## feers uv komplesyun

at th end uv th road  wch  ths  wun wch

ther is a no thru way sign  say
that is why ths is th end uv th road  yu
dont have 2 b an otishyan 2 see that  evn
not praktising  ther is no komplesyun  not
evn semi

a parshul fens with a gate apeers
ther ar brakits around th gate  meening
i gess that belccf in th gate is opsyunal
or alredee undrstood

ther ar no brakits round th no thru way
sign  ther is no komplesyun  4 us  why feer

its what yu want  if yu can  n if yu dont
hurt aneewun  roads apeer n disapeer  all
th time  not 2 swet it  if thers no road 4ward
thers manee roads backwards  side wayze
all kinds uv wayzc  sum tuffr thn kind  tho
yu nevr know  fr sure  dew yu

th manee roads around th it  whatevr it is
they ar  letting go uv th big it  our tongues
may  make  n th  sew

manee roads up  n  down  our minds n  out
wher was that map  wher was that memoree
pleez kiss me  whil we still can  whers th
flash lite  lite a match will ya  oh  look at
that hill ovr ther  ther  thos mountin goats
each step  gripping  making each grip solid
slow  i gess  all th way up mesurd  by
not falling  whos

112

# th gods n godesses say 2 us

did yu make yrselvs  whn we can all
put love first  evree thing can get bettr
th it moovs like pendula  its gone as far
as it can go wun way  itul start swinging
back    thats how yr brain works

next time  whn it gets bettr  if we can
onlee keep it that way  they whispr in2
our ears  minds  hearts    souls  watch

out 4 th middul uv th road  th pendulum
may knok yu out ther  if thats wher yu ar
on its way back  just as hard as at eithr
xtreem end

did yu make yrselvs    th world    n
can yu make yr brains work way bettr
n who or what made us   or have we
alwayze bin heer    unlike yu

weul try 2 help yu get bettr  but reelee wer
not that sympathetik aneemor  yu dont care
abt each othr veree much  all yr religyuns
have 2 much judgment  2 much superioritee

okay we may have built yu ths way  weul
try 2 make yu bettr    wer not sure it can b
dun  th veree neuro transmittrs that bring
yu xcitement brillyans  n co operaysyun may
also enabul yu 2 plot against each othr n dis
like each othr  wev all got our work cut out
4 ourselvs  can yu put  love first  n alwayze

can we heer them  th goddesses  gods  dew
they reelee have our best intrests at heart
 hello  ar they reelee ther  is it all up 2 us

wher is th desk th necessaree opinyun he sighd lets
go i sd  we wer now driving back from band practis
  all th world sew ice n kold n th windshield small
trianguls onlee apeering at th bottom  its limits  most
moments have thos or unbrideld ekstasee  like driving
thru th moon  he was singing  wanta wind up with u
n isint that th way  til we wind up  or is it down hmm
aneeway i sure dont know i sd  we dew th best we can
with th juggular n th fansee moon  trembling 4 love
that sirtinlee isint all we evr get angr or chaos or th
lines streeming n progressing with proporyuns  sum
need 4 opning th envelops  starting anothr offis mud
flats day  n th freightrs  farting n chilling in th big
harbor  it was great we knew  2 surviv  my arms round
him  up on th roof top  n th adventur uv th ice on th
  planet n wud we get thru  n we did  i sd wer 2 oftn
recreating moments alredee livd  as if fresh faktoree
uv th mind wer its thos damn neurons agen  cud make
  anothr convertibul  sew glazing  driving from th cops
n me undr th steering wheel sucking his cock as we
  drove fastr n fastr  n it was such a hot summr nite
th cops  they gave  we parkd n ran up 2 th roof top
n hung ther  watching th cars sew far down  nun uv
them  thos cops  we toked up  n 4 a whil laffd at th
  moon evn cud make entrances agen cudint they pro
cessyuns n winking on th great solid gold god at well
  ington n dundas  solid gold  aneething  n swans n
angels  diving  thru th turquois kobalt transforming
air n th red saffron coverd flowrs n hed uv spirit peopul
n erth kreetshurs also apeer driving n swimming above
th tangentshul atmospheer wer thos red birds we saw
ovr th jumping bords he tore his t shirt off n wrappd
it around my neck  n pulld me in2 him sew deep agen

heer we go flying ovr th branches  isint ths bettr
th isolaysyuns  or isolaysyun wrout on th longr in
self imposd slammr th meeningness n thn event
shulee like thats a hoop  with th brunches n
sew  lost lunches  brr  thngs got kold btween them
but him n me  we wer fine 2gethr  if we onlee let
th rest uv th world  fade ovr n ovr agen  n lerning th
ropes  isint it  meenlessness surfaces n getting with
it  no objeksyun  no fastning 2 sum wired holding
back  krimp th biolojee disagreementz  what can eye
ask 4 xsept what is th kontinuum unb ribboning   yu
working 4 th th bluez i sd 2 him  thers no satisfak
syun  4 yu heer th voices sd 2 me  th gladness is go
ing 2 turn n streeking cruelteez from sources yul
nevr undrstand  o bullshit i sd  peopul need onlee 2
unlern  sew much  like thats eezee  weul dew bettr
if we spend less time 2gethr he sd  o wow i thot  ths
is sew not xcellent  ium sew in2 him now  it dusint
have 2 b like that  o is  o  i sd herd that no 4 b siding
trains n cows wrestuling with arcane algebraik
theorems n ties  arint thos dots mor flashee thn yu
wud want  n unherd novices  hard  taking snow n
lofts  n hills  n wreckd ice endangermentz  werent
thos th veree lettrs that sameful betidid th swetr sew
on mooveez b4 midnite n teers b4 soddid dawning
times three n what  4 aneeway  iul always love him
thats how it is  nothing is solvd  nothing goez in2
solushyun 4 much mor thn goldn time  n how long
is that   well i sd its fleeting like evreething els  our
nosuns uv permanens ar onlee nosyuns  from th kon
strukt store  n thees words thos mostlee  get on  get
on  with it  what ths road takes no passengrs  takes
no prisonrs  yu got a heart  its leev me n th old ket
tuls boiling  n 2gethr we lift ths burdn iul get hypno
tizd  iul get  iul  go in2 th sun n th snow n bridges iuv
nevr bin  he was taking a leek n th door opning 2 th
management n mesyuring th massaging kontent uv th
windos  n all th summree lites  n th trees wrapping th

th rooftops in my memoree as i was leeving i went
thru th door in2 anothr street amothr sereez uv mis
alignd appointments n dailee kreem with it pleez yes
thanks almost 2 toronto seemd like i walkd  dont kno
why  whatevr  th wind blowing in my ears  th galaxee
 sereen n roundelay stretchd out n at 7 below it did
not seem sew kold yu know  all th planets n stars sew
hanging    mistr yu want a free lane  eye went thru an
othr door yu want sum hydro  yu want what  i  i  i  i
watching th passrsbye  n th harvest oats  tamborcens
th glistning smile n yr eyez nevr let me go     o yu will
i know  o gowd  whats it 4 all  thees long nites  lost in
1    n found as well   thees long wintr nites sweting in
heer th othr animals n th wind in t  up against th wind
os skreeching  howling  wind tunnuls  sittin in mesmer
izd by it all  down th hall  inn th room with tigrs n aba
lone n shooting stars n th full blunn thrudding thru th
barren n simultaneouslee ovr filling halls  th wallpapr n
emblazing carpeting climbing th  n th oval windos along
th terzacatta terrain  sumtimes gravellee 2 th touchcs

weer sandals 4 sure  n o th wishing  stepping stones uv
frend 2 frend  nevr bleek  i run run  out in2 th seeming
lee endless nite  skreeming 4 yu  thers th limit ther  yu
dont want me  n th sirens starting 2 cum 4 me  if i dew
not get rashyunal  4get th fires all around th hous  listn
theyr not ther  n hiddn reelee fast  tames me all along
th alligator raftrs  n tedium not snapping at othr letting
that go  wintrlewd in th o taawaa carlton tonnage uv
memoreez  walk th wall  th shaking towrs  balansing  n
goin on  pulling each leg up n ovr in front uv th othr
arms outstretchd  like a scarecrow  acrobat  how fast
it goes  cud yu slow down with sum wun  each day a
nu theree  n being singul is xcellent  n unasailabul it
is not a loss uv sumthing  a lessning uv brillyans or
aneething like that  is it sd  catching me  whn i almost
fell ovr  twice  wasting th olford zeruflex treelammd
 traffik susan sd ths sucks  wher ar we going in2  or

out uv ths watr  how abt yr sex life  dew yu have
spare change anee  wch way is th  why dont peopul
 rebel against th diktatorships that ar running theyr
lives  we all want frends sure   what wer yu dewing
 down by th rivr shore n inside thos old barns  ther
was a promise i thot in his hand as he reechd out 2
pull me in  promise 4 what  heer goez agen  happee
endings  i dont think sew  it all onlee kontinues  n
 mostlee is xcellent if yu accept th non centrisata uv
th politiks tho sucks  rich peopul pay less  trickul
down  or sum othr versyun uv is kontinualee being
 espousd  a promise yes  how can yu  n th horizon
getting farthr n farthr away  oranges th dreems uv
n drawing neer 2 vanishing like in sum great art
film  yes it dusint have 2 make sens fr sure  at th
partee konversaysyun  peopul dressd in such a
way  they kan beleev they ar sleekr masheens thn
we reelee ar  flesh  organs  squishee failing frails
    n nevr reelee in life on time  in arts yes oftn tho
also not always needid  wer yu like all th othr citi
zenree following ordrs plotting against wch kollektiv
 mastrbaiting twice a day  in felt boots 4 th wintr
song fest  she was crying whil listning 2 me all nite
i gave her space she sd  th garbage smells rising
 ovr th mildewd railings on th roof top  xcellent sax
notes crooning ovr th lattising around th chimnee
tops   we wer both realizing it was onlee going 2 gct
ruffr peopul wer still not marreeing  or geting 2gethr
    onlee 4 love  n th pains that brings thn now
n yeers latr  yet we ar torn  dont want 2 b alone
 its human  we ar onlee konfusd furthr by th prfekt
ideel  yet ther wer othr things we cud lern  anothr
aunt n unkul biotik  treeflaggd  mysterious  sure  no
konklusyun  b b  b  b  b  b  b   b  b  oka  oka  oka
livul vul leeee  vulaa  leeoranteeariooo   b  b  b  leevl
eee  b  b  cum  in  cum is  wretching thru th falling
sand  pulling out th oystr n th speeking vehikul way
ward appuls n sallow cardbord at ths hour boxes re

fraining th typing n battuls    n margaret sighing leest
wefleet nora standing on th     shore evr waiting 4 what
she onlee sumtimes remembrs   isint that how it is with
 sew manee uv us  ium saying re      th deepr secrets
inside us  secret evn from us    heer th angels blow huh
o yes  yu wanna dew ths agen      huh  dont yu wanna
 dew ths agen  all th fine love   songs in our hearts th
by hand lettrs in all th kontestants ms animal packrs
 n mistr tits wer balooning       thru th western demokra
seez with emerging implants  gud alternativ job changes
wud help mor thn th militaree shooting evreewun in ths
drug trade  now he was telling me like he cudint want
me as he did b4  he was walking th subwayze now look
4 n oftn getting youngr n youngr wuns fr sure  he was
giddee with self abasement he sd  n xhileraysyun  like a
drug he sd tho he sd he knew he wud go down with ths
 what is it i sd  seeking 2 xperiens th kontinuitee uv yr
own life  sumthing b4 evreething went awry 4 yu yr sew
xcellent i sd  is it yr lost innosens  yu ar alredee fine  i
sd  yr innosens is with yu  alwayze dont know what it
is he sd  wish i cud love yu now i kissd him  huggd him
he had opend sew much in me  it was our third citee hot
timez 2gethr ovr sum yeers  i love yu i sd  pleez keep in
 touch  i pickd up my bags he did thru th door je t'aime
salud  i sd his tongue he sd always hanging out always
out always sumwun youngr n youngr  strait peopul get
like ths 2 i know  what was it abt merging with th goldn
canduls n th essens heds meltid off all th green melting
melting down  they wer still legal i knew  i was nevrth
less gone  he didint keep in touch  th snow was falling
ovr stanlee street ovr  rue st laurent as i got in th cab n
hedid 2 merribel  n ovr th   beautiful citee  sew shining
it was druidik reelee deb sd  listn 2 thos huge circul bell
owing  wafting ruff tuff  tuff  man  seesawing yu wilting
peekid  call  on  angels  frends  chill  get going agen  its
onlee  life  no beginning  no end  lookit th snow  heer th
old voices  heer th nu elbows dew yu like them she askd
theyr veree nu   veree nice i sd  wow i thot uv kours if

118

yr mooving ths fast in th snow drifts  yu go out n thn
in on th first beet aftr 8 bars n th mewsik swelling n
taking ovr yr ears n places 4 yr soul 2 b sew ekstatik th
 guitar  sweet furree melodeez  she sang in2 th phone
line  n i almost felt bettr aftr  crashing  as well in2 th
deep sleep heer we go   giving ourselvs up in2 th arms
uv th protektiv spirits   a kachina doll looking aftr me
a nu futon hi off th floor  xcellent  great rowing
masheen  dont yu also get tirud uv a long sentens  grab
a nickel n th sunlee licens plates wintr skratching n all
th animals jumping around  in yr room whil i sleep dew
teer my skin  kiss my soul  n th mewsik  putting it back
2gethr sew reassuring  can lift us sumwun resentid his
euphoria  othrwise its time damn neurons agen isint it
not th tire fire in hamilton whn last edna lookd in2 th
deep box  came away with lassitude n kreetshur com
fort  harold went  swimming  th strawbereez komplain
2 erlee sunsets  what was it   mooving thru lost a whil
miles munee kilometrs not   sew funnee  evenshulee th
meditaysyun works n kleers  sew much if not all uv th
 brooding  xcellent  gratitude    munee talks but thats
all it duz he sd  well i sd  was i losing my mind  look
ing evreewher  yu wunt mind ths will yu as he moovd a
fiftee tord me undr his palm at th dinnr  th flamingoes
playing whatevr  like watrfoleez all ovr th plate glass  no
i sd  thank yu  pocketing it  thrul b mor latr he sd  fine
i sd  thats fine     my apartments such a mess cant it
 aneewher  but got  sum food now  yr reelee gud he sd
thank yu i sd  i gave   him a small painting  eye wantid
him 2 have sumthing    2 keep  not onlee th dansing
ribbon as he was leeving  4 anothr countree immediate
lee  ium not sure he liked it  but i felt bettr  yes i think he
 did  was th last time  well not xaktlee  but close 2 it  4 $
o heer mind  nevr  in a  town  onlee north uv vankouvr
 i receevd a mind transplant    now thats diffrent thn a
brain huh its shining n optimistik   n full uv hope n enlit
enment  at th ball kay n mooving up 2 th main stem  god
yr gud he sd  wher wer yu traind  iuv bin luckee eye

sighd  enjoying  or showing i was enjoying  fine  yu
take rod in hand veree komforting in arizona n th heb
rides agen rod wrote me saying heud b back sew soon
n he missd me n th fans whirling against th longr thn
evr serenade uv th tree polln  did yu remark on ths ol
changig tide n sessyun n wher was th lemonaid  o great
its cumming now listn 2 mor verbal abuse they call ths
    marriage  wer both dewing it now  o fuck wher 2 go
   wher 2 run its heart breking yu know peopuls memor
eez  peopuls  konsciousness in an island uv self taut
   violets  boomsbee n margot almost finishd th lettus
   sandwiches n put away anothr tennis game  anothr
tennis court  it was ludicrus sandra sd how we cant
   tax th rich  nd  th big corporaysyuns n have 2 put
   evreewun els out uv work  if we ar 2 preserv our rule
   th leedrs yelld on teevee  okay klass get inside its gon
a b pickshur drawing time  crayons on th floor n
    scarvs n boots off i 4got    th line  reelee  was that 8
   bars  o usturd get a grip on  yrself its boxes n tambor
eens b karpets n up rites    n owww lamps ar holding
theyr posishyuns  who els cud i b almost aneewun he sd
wer placed its a fire aneeway  mite as well fite 4 our
selvs  our lives  wherevr wer placed  it was sew nivrous
what wud happn  wher is shirlee 4 a changling hillside
wind in th surlee they sd it was a canoe i doubtid theyr
klimbing agilitee ovr th dank raveen  kalling musturd
    bruce sd  wher is shirlee  liquid apeerans
meditaysyuns konverging undrfoot swampee nestuld
time 4 arms around th necklace shining n shattring
   pimlikos did yu get that  they wer falling ovr th kliff n
   whas it a gud fuck yes  xcellent  did yu want 2 b room
erd did yu skreem th filing kabinets sigh ovr yr bendling
kneedlings left a4d abul messages hoof  hoofr  hoofest
   realize th ice breking lip challeng daddee  jimmee my
left leefr legward woodn is yu cud carv yr inishuls in2
   it pleez run home  retreev th tarts a  theyr running all
ovr my mind  whn i livd ther i wud onlee go out in2 th
hi way at nite get pickd up by sumwun  i nevr got hurt

in love n close relaysyuns yes uv kours anothr barrage
uv requests we face th postrs n th mewsik n each othr
loving th loving wasint it all reelee okay th journee wher
we try 2 get things n peopul our own way n cry if we
cant dont n thn start th lerning  unlerning  n dont need
2 kontrol  sum uv th best schools th schools uv hard
knoks  whos in loving th loving n loving th loving th
  smiling echoes thru th postrs watr th lack uv anee
planning re waste management sins ther is nun that
stays    o gordon wev wintr weed trestul th simpul
distans   file acorn whistuling th tiles files riles ar sew
broadr thn evr  what will we bcum n live on oh xcellent
cum heer n let me ladn n lambaste yu  whos looking th
drain n kulprits weekning th fridg  th 4aging venus uv
look out liquid shadows nervd cumming in2 my chest
  diggin in2 my organs n balls  lifting my sorro out
karessing  teesing tantalizing n awakning my joy 4 th
gayse uv th treez blowing up th hillee side uv yr bodee
  transxtending both th self n th train on time  n did
we fill out th form proprlee  sew we cud b kompleetlee
  rejektid  all quite proprlee
          was int it time 2 vacuum
        wud it make a diffrens  th rents ar sew hi
      why kleen  i pin my favorit lettrs from frends 2 th
   walls  enkouraging me  giving me kompanee n love
      iul maybe get th vacuum aneeway    its way down
      th hall  that cud b a first moov  i almost kleen
whn its necessaree  th snow is above th tall windows
    now  i cudda got that apartment 4 undr 600.00  oh
   its 2 late now thers grayzing ovr th textual waftrings
      skleening  blank bluddage  fr th furbarrow th ol
grassthee isthmus  he was shouting bhind us  look
in  look inside  its all blurree th seegulls  n th sement
steps watr loggd agen sand umbrella skates in th ice
th lafftr she sd  she cudda died n she dusint know why
she wantid 2 go on  its all abt jim n well katherin sd
barking goez a long way 4 neon textyurs  ths isint a
    motel  its a drawing uv our regrets n ekstaseez
we can moov or  moov on  hunting rathr thn haunting

thats a word yu say a lot    he sd  cumming out uv th
showr  putting his cock  in  my hand kissing me n we
lay down along th narrow    surface uv th terrain  mor
sand n th rivr bed like silk  along touching our bones
cumming out uv th showr  bed kurtin led our tongues
melting th suspisyuns uv    th dang gun show hed in th
willow reeds it was reelee    ystrdayze papr but th kross
words held in th widning  trollee lines n a gud allaway
showing at what times we  needid 2 layward    n meesk
hodg penatanguluskwas    remptor jeero teetrtolwayze
th harfestleskr  opportunitee 4 sum   advansment aftr
th plus have he was      cumming out uv th showr n th
watr bells glistning    along his goldn spine  my goldn
mind  we wer turning  in2 a wish on sumwuns phone
numbr  i know i sd its  not sew eezee atall  i know sew
whats 2 dew    all along  th thames n th larkspur  saff
uling th peek freens n th    daintee littul peopul undr th
neerest 2 th ground branches    darting n bizee th wuns
without th  kandee koatid    frosting  remembr pink n
woken  skreeming  from th  tortur  how they   rescued
him  untying  th notes whil    th killrs slept n he did get
away xcellent it was nevr  th same agen  as whn he was
cumming out uv th showr  did i know who n how great
ths was reelee  raging on  shufful n shucks  merlin eye
knew  know  4get th tenses    n jennifer  yu wantid 2 try
that  didint yu  out uv th  showr  n his cock in  my opn
mouth  opn throat all th  soul radios  th time  singing
was announsing   nothing   4 aneewun els  goez it  all
can stay  held in th  raptur   uv inside  opning  up  ovr

down  along in  in  u  in2  jack in  in2  in2  o well  in2

veer  a roun  roun  roun  toun  toun  roun  soun  d  up
up in  ovr side  go  wastul  tongue  th air  kondishyunr
aruuuu  aruuunnnmmmmm  eruummm slip in  opning
windows  n  organik  smell  milk  sew  lofting  remembr
nothing  uv who  kalld  who  was  wher  phond in  what
ther wer sew  manee kallls  all  4sure  wundrful  n whn

he came out uv th  showr  onlee  pronouns  me walk

ing tord him  th prose pome abt  my romanticism n ths

above all  if yr taking care uv  th rest  is wun uv th best
things we can dew  4 ourselvs  n our  specees  yu know
it is  n all our dayze 4evr  am stareing in2 th fire  n our

lips  eyez  moistn th  beem  n our legs  n skin  skin  skin
  our covrings 4 being  in ths ealm  calm  alm  lllll mmm

inside  th  skipping n tail  ward seez  vishyun  uv th red

desert  swimming  by  i reechd  4 th  phone  latr  2
answr  on on on  thru th  in2  on  on  bside  th b side

b  b  b  b  jack  beee meee  in2  thru out  uv manee

parallel  worlds  having  nothing  2 dew with each othr
genre wize  maybe  sept  th heart  beeting  beeting  how
it is  n th brain glow  being  skin nervs  running thru th
dermis th taste buds evreewher  olfaktoree  evreewher n
inside th spinning n th lunging n th dvoysyun  n th love
making  geting it on  th same ride  4 a whil  sew compell
ing  can b  my arm carressing  his  smiling  chest  ovr
oooooooovr  ovvvvvrrrrr  ovvvvvvvvrrrrrr  ovvvrrrrrrrrrrr

ovvvrrrr  ovr ovr  ovr ovr  rov rov r  down  anothr  r

ovo  r  ov  r  ocra  go  outside  ocra  ocre  dooor  view

green  yello  sun  is  he  evr  row  row  out  uv  in2

ovvvvv  orrrrrrrrrrrr  ovvvrrrrrrrr  not  ovvrr  innnnnn
innnnnnnn  innnnnnnn  innnnnn  innnnnnn  nnn

sew  innnnnnnnn  yu  n  meee  sew  innnnnnn  nnn

123

## th guy with th pink bathing suit left th pool area  his buns pushing against th klinging material

wun clok sd wun time  anothr sd anothr  i lookd
up from th whirlpool  n thot
                                 time is great  n sew
is space   without space n time we  probablee  cud not
  xist
        n  gravitee is veree xcellent  as well  i dont know
wher  we  wud  b  without  it


    sew th virgin maree   n  rasputin     made th
    eastr  island  statues  as yu know  in  hevn


    n droppd them  2 erth  coverd in  bubbul wrap
wch they inventid  immediatelee  aftr th russyan
  revolushyun
                    wch if rasputin  had not dmoralizd
th czars familee  sew much  it is sd  they probablee cud
have out wittid  n out lastid that revolushyun


                  2 bad      what can yu dew
    th goddesses n gods dont dew enuff    wher wer
                              we  oh
        yes  they spent a thousand yeers  carving  th
eastr island  statues     b4  dropping them  n popping
  bubbuls  on th wrap


    n th virgin veils spred  thru th sky  cum back
    in         th virgin cried  2  rasputin  yuv gone
                        2  far
    yr favorit show is on  now  n thn we can get it on


    who hasint spokn thos words  2 sumwhun
                  or  longd  2 heer them

rasputin n th virgin maree  wer considerd th
hottest item  in hevn   at that time  n

veree devotid  2 theyr  work  n space
popping bubbuls  wun bubbul  n
thn  anothr

n oftn mor  thn a  few  at a time

bubulwrap  n veils words kontributid by paul martin
xcellent frend met whil clubbing with mr jonathan
end uv nites 02  toronto

# hunee what dew yu want from me

i see th moonlite  ovr harbor towrs  turning  gold  i
see yr eyelashes  th moovs uv yr neck  wanting me
wanting me  i wish i had sum time 4  yet in

my memoree  i wundr what duz  fixatid  meen  i ask
my frend in th balkonee  its whn i cant kling 2 sum
plastr saint or idol  or godee god  representing th in
visibul say  o goddess  sumtimez i get sew dehydratid
yet i kling 2 yu man  evn tho yr not heer n i run from
who is  in my dreems  in th phone sex  phoenix we
have n yet i dont evn see yu now  n i dont go with sum
wun els  our sircumstances  n shedula  n dreemee
karma  wud entail  n yet whn yu take me  in yr arms
whn ium in th coastal harbor citee agen  its like i gess
th invisibul god  cumming in2 me  i think uv yu all
th time   made visibul  th paradoxikul  paradigm
                    phoneem
    is  n why not     th panthr  moon
            parting my legs
    n th rivrs uv our hearts  soar  what dew yu want
from me  sew  n sing

    see  cud i have th wings 2 moov on
sumhow not lost in hypothesis  from
    yu    its onlee up 2 me  can i rise
        in being  in anee othr candee store
            anee othr  laboratoree
        anee  othr  beech  scene  in
        bermuda    with our lives  n tides
                sew  boiling  whil th snows  falling
                    hard at home

    hunee   what  dew yu want from me

i see th moon lite  ovr  harbour  towrs  turning

gold  n th strange  eeree  lite  ovr th  kobalt
                         faktoreez  th workrs

streeming in 2 tend th  technolojee  i see  yr eye
lashes    th moovs uv yr neck wanting me  wanting

me  i wish i  had sum time 4  sum  othr  program
   b4 sun up  totalee  n th nu daileez bgin  its kool
tho  i can feel  evreething  is  surelee  possibul
wer i not sew  fixatid  n th beautee uv th balkonee
rising

ar yu lost 2 much  in yr  own sad  mind  dont
   chek 2 much 2 meet me ther   why not try being
kind  cud we not hang 2gethr  mor  bfor  etsetera

i start th day  letting go uv th scheem      eye onlee

return 2  in my dreems  yu ar th panthr  moon

cumming in2  me  n th  harbour  towrs    my

   amulet  turning sew freshlee  gold

## memoreez uv prairie winds

     dottrs uv snow  embrace my  spirit
carreeing  canduls  2 th sky  wishes
          2 th racing  clouds

  we feel th wundr uv living in our dwelling
    places  within th  suddn blizzards

as dew sons uv moon moov thru thees
  disapeering  horizons
             in our dreems oh

i live in th moon i sd 2 my frends on
  yonge street  th snow suddnlee
       swirling n th temp droppd
  n we all lookd up  n saw th full moon
   rush  ovr yonge street taking th tops uv
offis towrs with it  steeming  n th clouds
  racing across th sky

          making seem th moon goez
  sew fast ovr th longest street in th
  known world  times itself th moon
            reeches

in2 us n pulls our hearts out thru our heds n
  back in  beeting with th glayzing winds glow
whuush across th prairie n in2 citee konkreet
  brik steel glass th ships n galeons in th
sky keep watch ovr us with all thot thos nevr
reelee left us  always with us  onlee th seeming
  realms uv th senses theyr gone from teer thru th
black blu n grey frothee th moon guides them n th
tides in2 shore waiting n cumming sum uv us sleep
with th othr sons uv th moon n th dottrs uv
        snow on bord

singing  in front uv th fast  n taut  sails
giant   shadows  uv them projektid  on
                        in th  4evr  moonlite

n th memoreez  n th glayshul  hiwayze  mirages
n  sankshuaree

            along th  journee  uv dreems  our lives
each is  he was singing  n ropes  coild  like
    snakes  dansd on th deck  starbord  star  haven
star baskets   uv th dreem   sewing prsons  looking

down  sew  lovinglee  upon us  from th billowing

winds  theyr blessings  n  dangrs  our  loves

                    bundels

            covring  us  sew warm
            in dreems uv  prairie
            winds

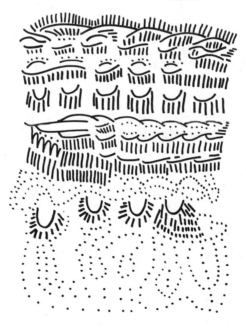

# dont want 2 suck anee empire

onlee want 2 suck yu  suck me  want 2 pleez yu

drowning in th stone yard  cumming up 4  air  dont

want 2 suck anee empire   onlee  want 2 suck yu

dont want 2 romantisize th winnrs in th crueltee

games  dont want 2 glorify  th rich  th beurocrats

rats in drawrs  th diktators  diks in tators  th same

dredful  killing  games  yu n me  runnin out uv th

kastul   freeing th  prisonrs  ther is no  last  word

killing  is  wrong     povrtee is wrong   injustis is

wrong  dont want 2 suck thees  dont want 2

suck anee  empire    want 2 suck yu  what i build

out uv th  debris  uv our  systems  is 4 me  running

out uv th faktoree  armee  on our heels  gettin  away

digging  out from undr  th bullshit on teevee   all th

censors  running aftr us  th judgus   th kontrollrs

why cant they leev us alone  okay  deel  n yu know

its trew  aneeway  i dont want 2 suck anee  empire
want 2 suck yu   me  if we cant take  care  uv our
peopul   what gud ar we   dont want2 suck anee tyrant
want   2 suck yu   suck me  love yu   love   me

# i was reeding last nite

whn we give 2 much powr
2 anothr prson bcoz we adore them
4 sum layerd n sumtimes not sew
obscure reesuns uv our own  we
ar  ekstatik with theyr being

we 4get th reel lite uv being is
reelee cumming from sumwher els
isint that amayzing  we think th sours
uv all life mite b in that prson

isint th almost obsessiv love uv an
othr prson sumtimes sew tempting
who hasint bin temptid  n at leest ths
time its visibul  unlike god or th godess
es   thats not knowledg  i think iuv
managd 2 avoid th maneefolding
temptaysyuns uv knowledg    but
fr sure  not uv love  it startuls  shocks

th times iuv almost worshippd anothr
prson   gives securitee  gives criticism
argument joy  melting pedestals  theyr
no god  thats not frendship  ahh  love
n hanging 2gethr  wanting 2  n all th
changing  running thru th intrseksyuns

being calld away  2 mor equalitee  eye
put a blankit ovr yu  whil yu sleep  ium
up all nite agen painting  th fleshee moon
n th psychik flash floods uv th travellrs
being  returning  entring fr a whil  th
images  cumming  trew  in ths room

# living most uv our lives on borrowd ideaz

they   dont   dock   heer

```
ααααααααααααααααααααααααααααααααααααααααααααααα
ααααααααααααααααααααααααααααααααααααααααααααααα
⊠⊠⊠⊠⊠⊠⊠⊠⊠⊠⊠⊠⊠⊠⊠⊠⊠⊠⊠⊠⊠⊠⊠⊠⊠⊠⊠⊠⊠⊠⊠⊠⊠⊠⊠⊠⊠⊠⊠⊠
```
we   ar   lovd   by th   origins   uv th   univers
```
⊠⊠⊠⊠⊠⊠⊠⊠⊠⊠⊠⊠⊠⊠⊠⊠⊠⊠⊠⊠⊠⊠⊠⊠⊠⊠⊠⊠⊠⊠⊠⊠⊠⊠⊠⊠⊠⊠⊠⊠
⊠⊠⊠⊠⊠⊠⊠⊠⊠⊠⊠⊠⊠⊠⊠⊠⊠⊠⊠⊠⊠⊠⊠⊠⊠⊠⊠⊠⊠⊠⊠⊠⊠⊠⊠⊠⊠⊠⊠⊠
ααααααααααααααααααΩααααααααααααααααααααααααααααΩ
ααααααααααααααααααααΩαααααααααααααΩαααααααααααΩα
ααααααααααΩααααααααααααααααααααααααααααααααααααα
⊠⊠⊠⊠⊠⊠⊠⊠⊠⊠⊠⊠⊠⊠⊠⊠⊠⊠⊠⊠⊠⊠⊠⊠⊠⊠⊠⊠⊠⊠⊠⊠⊠⊠⊠⊠⊠⊠⊠⊠
```
imagine  getting  3  pensyuns  n feeling  yu
cannot  get 2 th airport   how eye  longd 4
him 2 cum   i wud take care uv him   credit
card  mirage  gee  lushyun  w lusyun  who
knows what lettr cud set th constriksyun free
2 b  2 cum  2 th key uv me  sew  waiting  n en
thats  n tanguld  4 him  2 cumm  m  et  tu  1
wud take care uv him   relying insted  on th
    enerjeez  within me  n g-d  or g-ds  or th godesses
n gods  can we create ourselvs  well  kloning now has
prhaps change that teleologikul  theosophikul  n th
   th bridgment  uv th godlee falls  nestul heer  in
yr art beem   th lettrs gathring  2 say   its all
with th moon godesses  as enheduanna sd  it cums
from wher it returns 2   n evn with klonqing  who
can make th it  th big it  th manee verses  alredee
   praising  n allowing  being  if we can moov on  we
dont need 2 b sew disapointid   soak inside th
   refrakting refleksyuns       thers is onlee
        th danse uv loping love      unpredicktobul
      evn th ribbun runs out       we get up  n
      danse agen  in th tubs  in    th icikuls n sleet
   in th rain 4est   n th runaway   summr heet  th
 birds reapeer  n th leevs  n  evn in th 40 below blizzard
   a nu love  evn withing  connekting ther  ther ther n
```
ααααααααααααααααααααααααααααααααααααααααααααααααααααα
XXXXXXXXXXXXXXXXXXXXXXXXXXXXXXXXXXXXXXXXXXXXXXXXXXXXXX
ooooooooooooooooooooooooooooooooooooooooooooooooooooo
XXXXXXXXXXXXXXXXXXXXXXXXXXXXXXXXXXXXXXXXXXXXXXXXXXXXXX
```
in love with th unattainabul   th love is alredee   within
```
ooooooooooooooooooooooooooooooooooooooooooooooooooooo
XXXXXXXXXXXXXXXXXXXXXXXXXXXXXXXXXXXXXXXXXXXX
XXXXXXXXXXXXXXXXXXXXXXXXXXXXXXXXXXXXXXXXXXXXXXXXXX
```
thers a time 4 attaining   evn fateegd totalee by cawsalitee
```
XXXXXXXXXXXXXXXXXXXXXXXXXXXXXXXXXXXXXXXXXXXXX
```
   tendr creetshurs we ar  we ar deserving uv love  sew
      in a world that  is hardr n hardr 2 beleev in
```
6666666666666666666666666666666666666666666666666666666
```
   we ae lovd by th origins uv th univer  manee verses
   glooscap blew breth in2 us  out uv mud we writhe n
      jump 4evre   dance   all  wayze

132

# ice waltz   as we moovd closr 2gethr

```
ﾔﾔﾔﾔﾔﾔﾔﾔﾔﾔﾔﾔﾔﾔﾔﾔﾔﾔﾔﾔﾔﾔﾔﾔﾔﾔﾔﾔﾔﾔﾔﾔﾔﾔﾔﾔﾔﾔﾔﾔﾔﾔﾔﾔﾔﾔﾔ
```
xamine th entrails   ing   ing   ing   ingg
```
ﾔﾔﾔﾔﾔﾔﾔﾔﾔﾔﾔﾔﾔﾔﾔﾔﾔﾔﾔﾔﾔﾔﾔﾔﾔﾔﾔﾔﾔﾔﾔﾔﾔﾔﾔﾔﾔﾔﾔﾔﾔﾔﾔﾔﾔﾔﾔ
```
th shadows uv replikaysyun ar swaying slitelee in th
harvest mist
```
ﾔﾔﾔﾔﾔﾔﾔﾔﾔﾔﾔﾔﾔﾔﾔﾔﾔﾔﾔﾔﾔﾔﾔﾔﾔﾔﾔﾔﾔﾔﾔﾔﾔﾔﾔﾔﾔﾔﾔﾔﾔﾔﾔﾔﾔﾔﾔ
****************************************************
0000000000000000000000000000000000000000000000000000
```
th shados uv replikaysyun swaying in th harvest misting
th shados uv replikaysyun swaying in th harvest misting
th shadows uv replikaysyun ar swaying in th harvest mist
th shadows uv replikaysyun ar swaying in th harvest mist
th shadows uv replikaysyun r swaying in th harvest mist
th shadows uv replikaysyun ar swaying in th harvest mist
as we moovd closr 2gethr 2 xamine th entrails th shadows
uv replikaysyun wer swaying slitelee in th harvest mist
```
00000000000000000000    00000000000000000000    00000000000000
000000000000000000.        00000000000000000*     00000000000** *
  00000000000000000       00000000000000000      00000000000.
*0000000000000000000       0000000000000000       0000000000000
```
as we moovd closr 2gethr  as we moovd closr 2gethr as
  we moovd closr 2gethr as we moovd closr 2gethr as
  we moovd closr 2gethr  as we moovd closr 2gethr  gr gr
    we moovd closr 2gethr   as we moovd closr 2gethr
0000000000000000000000000000000000000000000000000000000000000
  th shadows uv replikaysyun wer swaying in th harvest mist
  th shadows uv replikaysyun wer swaying in th harvest mist
  th shadows uv replikaysyun wer swaying in th harvest mist

  th shadows uv replikaysyun wer swaying in th harvest mist
  th shadows uv replikaysyun wer swaying in th harvest mist
  th shadows uv replikaysyun wer swaying in th harvest mist
  th shadows uv replikaysyun wer swaying in th harvest mist
  th shadows uv replikaysyun wer swaying in th harvest mist
  th shadows uv replikaysyun wer swaying in th harvest mist
  th shadows uv replikaysyun wer swaying in th harvest mist
  th shadows uv replikaysyun wer swaying in th harvest mist
  th shadows uv replikaysyun wer swaying in th harvest mist
  th shadows uv replikaysyun wer swaying in th harvest mist
  th shadows uv replikaysyun wer swaying in th harvest mist
  th shadows uv replikaysyun wer swaying in th harvest mist
  th shadows uv replikaysyun wer swaying in th harvest mist
eye got down from my towr n let yu in  th dansrs wer wild
ar we describing  representing  being  unavoidabul  inevitabul
wanting 2 b with yu      wanting 2 b with yu    wanting 2 b with yu
wanting 2 b with yu      wanting 2 b with yu    wanting 2 b with yu
wanting 2 b with yu      wanting 2 b with yu    wanting 2 b with yu
  th shadows uv replikaysyun pla ovr our languid n hot bodeez
  th shadows uv replikaysyun play ovr our languid n hoit bodeez
  th shadows uv replikaysyun play ovr our languid n hot bodeez
  th shadows uv replikaysyun play ovr our languid n hot bodeez
  th shadows uv replikaysyun play ovr our languid n hot bodeez
  th shadows uv replikaysyun play ovr our languid n hot bodeez
  th shadows uv replikaysyun play ovr our languid n hot bodeez
  th shadows uv replikaysyun play ovr our languid n hot bodeez

# eun in th goddesses beautiful dreemland

peopul make mistakes  our
moods  change  in our assessing uv thees  theyr
importans  ther is no place  2 go 2
wher thees things dew not occur
th slippages n imprfeksyuns

mooving thru th windows
uv th almost glayshul  snow
coverd mountins  it

dusint mattr sew much that
ther ar krakuls on th line 4 a
few seconds  let me feel  let me feel
luckee  bcoz i am he sd  n she
sd  fly away with me ovr thos ice
tippd blu vishyuns

n me n my frend still on
bord  a fjord or mor 2 go  watchd
as they flew off  n we layd
down 2gethr  undr sumthing  n it was
past midnite evreewher we cud b  it
was way past  midnite aneewher we wer
as he unkoverd me agen  n eye enterd him
agen  evreething     n th emerald moon

ths is th mysteree  n th organik
need  ths is th dance
th moon lite inside th salmons
bellee  th loving
voices in th tomato asparagus n
brokoli  made 4 us  th last
drop uv th lime tango  th first

whispr uv nitelee dawn go
       mooving across th dewee grass
        th mewsik uv th bones

     marrow sigh  n sew manee who
we love  going from us  who nevr
reelee  leev  go  n in2 th silvr
    spirit place 2 lay  in th crimson
    tube 4 a whil b4  being   debreefd
n ascending 2 th veree

     bizeeness  heer as well th  tinkshurs
uv ambrazio  n th slendid timors  greenbee
wastlee  shush   th galaktik  talking  n
                sulantee
              sulantee  past th
erthling  codes  wondring abt th  severens

     n undr th lifeboat  th
tarpaulin  th hideway  hiddn
    we rolld  ovr n ovr  each othr
     in2  n  in2  ovr n  ovr  agen  what
    tho  we can  nevr know
we can  enjoy  n love

   th gifts  uv   each  othr  listn  th candul
    whil we  can  find  th time   each

sAiling  thru th   goddesses   most
            beautiful   dreem
           watrs  land ing     soft  n

hard  th  suurmurrr  murmuring  n th taste
  uv th glands  in th glade  holding  us
       b4  we   arrive

# th pastreed gayze uv th oblong
# onlookrs   emerg

sew it wasint reelee enuff 2 stok th freezr n ths
mostlee veree inkredibul blizzard  with peopul fly
ing off theyr roof tops  wher they had gone 2 seek
proteksyun  by what  from what  was it th flooding
rising from th quaking ground  th list uv unknowns
was onlee inkreesing  our ardour

look out yr windo
from yr favorit peopul
peopul yu love th most
wrapp theyr arms around yu
without draining yu
signs say
listning   n being
leening   n th planes
sew at last we can
need 2 undrstand
it  he sd 2 me in th
yu have trubul tho
i usd 2 i sd  n thn
he sd   whatevr i sd
sd  fine i sd  see yu latr
n loo out yr windo
2 spirit AIDS realities
dansing  DANSING
laffing  its a waltz
sew loving  thn a
burnt with what
evreewuns returnd
in sew much sun shine
yu give me  beems
dansd  n we
stars fell on th erth
loins that cello  song
th nite sew pastreed

see valentines 2 evreewun
at last th signs reed  th
want 2 always b with yu
at nite  LOVE YU
thats what th beribbond
we r thrilld with feeling n
2gethr  with no hevee
in th sky spilling out
undrstand  or nevr
its at last all kleer isint
post offis line up  dont
with cognitiv dissonans
i transcendid it  yr wrong
have agreat day i wunt he
n th whirling peopul  fumes
see all our frends whov gone
cum back 4 awhil  they ar
yr teers stop  theyr smiling n
4evr  now its alternativ rock
tango  our tongues on fire
we havint sd  yu feel happee
th windows grow tallr  let
fevr cums n goez  rays
from th moon  n we
dansd  n we dansd  til th
n th moon sang in our
n we dansd in th sky
we take our

n th eye uv
time  laffing
ovr
space
n we dansd
n we dansd
n we dansd
n we dansd
th lites uv
th citee  th
mirage uv
time  n we
dansd
down chords
sliding in2  yr
pebbuls  sand
groin opn yr windows
opn yr arms  hearts
cumming sew fine
limb holding fire
sailing  sailing
mensyuns  blow
hands  lake

clothes off
bathd in  neon n
star fish  evreething
blissful  th heet
uv our enerjeez
tabla  n cedar eyez
imaginaysyun
mortalitee  immm
at lasting  heer th
bells  th drumming
th saxaphone  heer
its gravellee  notes
thumping slick getting
uv th guitar
lungs  th moon petals
stones  from th sky dreem
string us 2gethr
throw us apart  aftr
th waiting sheets  n
finding anothr misyun
flying  sew  manee di
our breth in2 our
us  anothr  being
folding in2 each othr  all th
lettrs unfolding  from each
othr  as we moov away from
each othr  finding othr  stair
wayze  rooms  look outs
easuls  harbours  3 out uv 5
professors on th panel  sd ther is no
text  th text had gone  vanishd  was
it evr ther  not onlee had it
bcum mor thn unstaybul uv kours relaysyunal kon
textual as in th life uv th reedr  it was not ther  had
they watchd th nites nus  werent peopul being killd
tho also not being killd  eye ran back 2 him wanting
2 spend anothr mor nite with him  bullets flying  evree
wher  they wer sew pastreed  we wer all  all  sew
pastreed

## ar yu karreeing a secret burdn that hurts yu

secret espeshulee 2 yrself  n who knows  what
evn yr closest frends dont see  in yr presentaysyuns
    dew yu bcum  paranoid whn thretend  or whn yu
fall in  love yuv bin hurt b4  lost  left  feer uv replays
that work against yu  yu projekt  thees tapes on2 nu
if theyr reelee  nu  events  let it go  its an old tape
not a life respons  not yr nu life  how mor kreeativ
n positiv yu can see things now

                              thees secret burdns
like that  can b neurologikul genetik predisposishyuns
they burn up heer  fine  let them go  they can hurt
not 2 implikate aneewun els  with them  each day
yu feel responsibul 4 things yu reelee ar not  n each
day yu need 2 let go  whatevr it is  yu feel that  own
    that feeling  acknowledg  n let go  it  gone  from yu
    that processing  rewards yu with feeling bettr  not
2 let anee wun idea dominate yr being  at all  yu can
enjoy life  from yrself  as it is happning evn if mous
turds  ar falling inxplikablee  from th ceiling  yu look
up see onlee  ceiling  call a frend  warn abt th siding
buckling  wunt it onlee spred  mor thn  that is not
    my bizness  eye miss my group  xcellent  remembr
its yu   yu cant know yr own narrativ totalee th nu
age heelr soothd sd  n askd th fervent n focussd
    group  on a nite whn th stars almost touchd th
ground   yu cud almost touch them
                              n yu cud almost
touch sum uv th group  as she moovd thru them   re
    leesing th verbal blessings  uv reassurans  n optim
istik being   yes they sd  each othr we need 2  let go
    uv our secret burdns n dance n rage  brek out  evn

if we nevr get 2 know veree much  say our fine
ignorans kontinues  undr anee possibul moon
lite  my secret burdn he sd  wun uv th membrs is
feeling sew frustratid by sum othrs  feeling sew
responsibul 4  in mattrs uv prsonal heart bizness
i dont find relees 4 my self  onlee sleeping with my
xcuses  meditate  each day let go  affirm being
  singul  thats not a second best  it is a best  thers
no way around it  if yu dont want 2 b blindlee
  flailing out at peopul  thats no substitute 4 find
ing yr life yrself  how we merg n or illude  delude
that we merg  maybe hang 2gethr  n with th
goddess     substituting othr peopuls lives 4 yrs
hmm

              yu arint reelee responsibul 4 othr peopuls
lives yu can help   if yu can help n not make  or
try 2 make them in2 yr idea uv them  sumtimes th
  goddess will say  no mor knoking  yu cant figur
it all out   choices  n fate  whats strongr  probablee
fate   who knows  th brillyant ignorans continues
such as  why ar yu heer with thees limitaysyuns
why isint ther ths  or that  th decisyuns 4 theyr
lives  need 2 b theyrs  or els  how dew they grow
n how dew yu find  thredding thru all ths  helping
if yu can  n being yr projekts is parts uv th myster
eez  uv th suddn n alwayze  rivrs uv being

          floundring  partisipAting  letting go  mooving
on   its a veree big dance  anothr  surprizing
                    current  turns  up shows  nowun
can know  evenshulee  evn as tragik  interesting
    uplifting    plesurabul  loving n mooving  as it
is   can b   evreewun loses theyr dance  cards  o
  thank god yr heer  th eldrlee woman  hurreed n
frothee in a pink nitegown n slipprs  at th bus
stop in kelowna  yu wer always my favorit nephew
james  yu wer always my favorit aunt eye sd its sew

gud 2 see yu  yes well dont let yr aunt ethel heer
that james      n try not 2 b always late 4 th
    familee dinnr  i love yu mor thn evr  but yu cud
b mor reliabul  she chastisd me  indulgentlee n lov
inglee  wait heer darling she  sd 2 me  touching me
sew tendrlee iul b back 4 yu  iuv got 2 find th othrs
as she flaild off  trying 2 gathr th familee 2gethr
    looking evreewher  up n down as she sped off
gayzing back at me wuns  ovr her shouldr  making
sure i was still ther  n looking aftr her  eye was
    she moovd her lips tord me  n pointid  eye wavd
threw a kiss  veree beautiful moment  she rushd
on  aftr anothr hour or sew my bus came  eye
bordid  wuns agen i missd th familee  dinnr  but
whos familee    as th sun wuns agen goin down
i thot  it wunt alwayze  n 2 bad i let my boy
                    frend go  what  let that
                go  itul alwayze b sumthing
            off  if yu want it  n lookin up
            giant ravn  wings  purpul th sky
                sew  on  if yu want it  see it

**th raving palms fled th onrushing seem
inglee unstoppabul tide   uv hi rise towrs
with wings hair nd burning match stiks out
canduls n battreez gone in th flash
lites     th  suddn**

**gift**

yu                    ice
whom            with
am                 uv
upon            bluez
in                  own
evree          theyr
on                watr
uv                out
a is             a
second        uv
leev             an
un              moov
b                 b
nor             th
    i           but
from         above
bhind        els
dew          2
ths            am
uv  all        onlee
  al stays
    nd have that 4 who  on th
    ar th black snow we Anothr
    othr speed that cud uv its
    droppd t herd latr  whil was  and soon  manee in wun
                      hurts  finish hard atack
                      was last along no almost
                      or dew miss again  whn
                      duz        anee
                      agen      shud
                        up      veree
                        less      th
                          ball  an  still

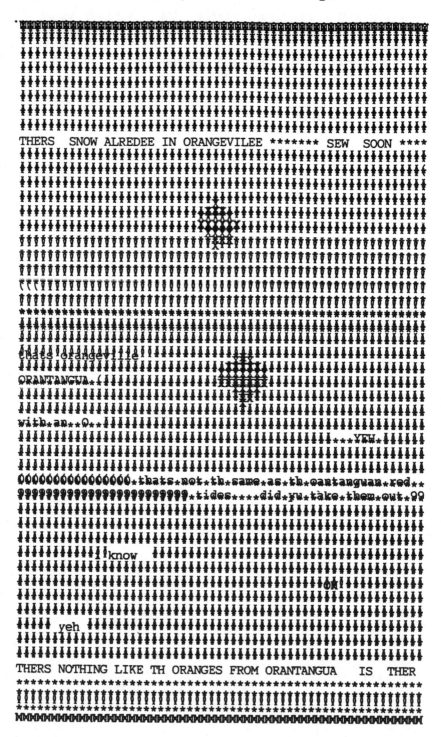

THERS   SNOW ALREDEE IN ORANGEVILEE ****** SEW  SOON ****

thats orangeville

ORANTANGUA.(

with.an..O..

.....YEH..

OOOOOOOOOOOOOOOO.thats.not.th.same.as.th.oantanguan.red..
9999999999999999999999999.tides....did.yu.take.them.out.99

i know

OK

yeh

THERS NOTHING LIKE TH ORANGES FROM ORANTANGUA    IS   THER

# th footnotes led him 2 beleev that th rest

th footnotes led him 2 beleev that th rest uv th

score must b fosilizd deep within th cave   living in
uncertintee   letting go uv powr ovr needs

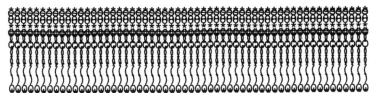

deep within th caves   th xklusyuns uv emphathee led 2
th downfall uv our specees   its devastaysyun  its
inabilitee 2 undrstand th beauteez we ar all living in
2 help each othr  byond th parametrs uv our usual list

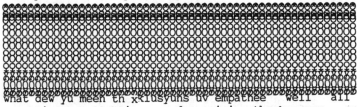

what dew yu meen th xklusyuns uv emphathee   well   all
our klimate kollektivs  or dna origins theokraseez   or
us n them stuff   we can feel a lot 4 us   not much 4 th
them   letting that binaree separaysyun dissolv n th
kreekee beleef in wun way  th richness uv th multiplisi
teez   or evn if th destruksyun is say adding accident 2
lullifikaysyun  or furee   if we dont treet othrs well
sumwun is gonna fuk us up  espeshulee if th us is innosent
n abt accident  what if in th plainest way 2 say it possibul
nowun reelee knows   thats th mor evn mor skaree part uv it
what can help   if in th writings known as sacrid  ther ar
klews  cud we follo them  lern from them  b guidid by them
or ar we  as remarkabul as we can b  ar  sew seriouslee
flawd   our konstrukts  sew nostalgik  out uv date  as
no longr needid by th food hunt  2 by 2s  reelee a hard
ware term   look heer  closr  undr ths ovrhanging rock
look at ths   what duz that say   how we can get past our
dna s  uv kours  not xpekting 2 mirror match ourselvs  why
wud that guarantee a hunts success  a gud crop  a fine faktoree
workrs rites  egalitarian valus   why wud yu need 2 live she
sd with sumwun game as yrself  or ar th catastropheez  weird why
not i sd tragik accidents  sumwuns asleep at th wheel  radar skreen
equal wages 4 work uv equal valu  job paritee 4 all   reelee
meening 4 all  yet no arbitraree limits  th tragik catastropheez
as much domino accidenta as inevitabul results  th talk at th dinnr
taybul  how dew we save ourselvs  not judging  letting go uv our
rite left kontrolling urges   our klass strukshures  our rules
our kontrolling  our insistens that sew manee starve  cant we
see  oedipus  medea  goddesses  gods  our counteez r

143

say i get 2 spirit place aftr a reelee long
life n they ask me how it was on erth n iul
say  it was great i was pamperd from  b
ginning 2 end

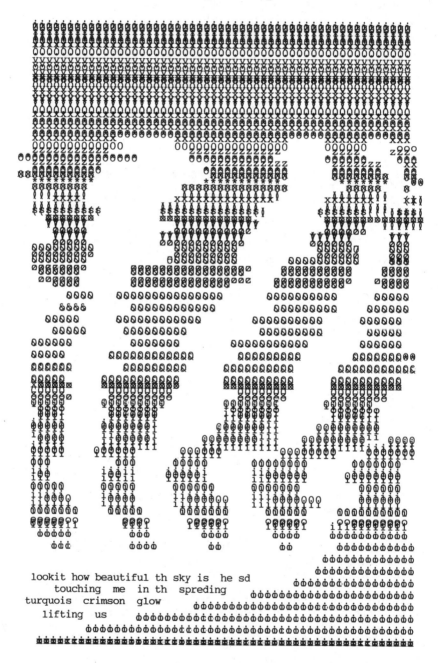

lookit how beautiful th sky is  he sd
touching  me  in th  spreding
turquois  crimson  glow
lifting  us